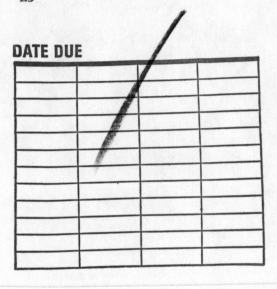

Twayne's United States Authors Series

Sylvia E. Bowman, *Editor*

INDIANA UNIVERSITY

John Cotton

JOHN COTTON

by EVERETT H. EMERSON
Florida Presbyterian College

Twayne Publishers, Inc.   ::   New York

FOR

K, AND S TOO

Preface

NO OTHER AUTHOR in American literature reveals so much about the nature of American Puritanism as does John Cotton, and the importance of Puritanism in American cultural history can scarcely be exaggerated. The habit of introspection, idealism, a profound awareness of sin, a demanding morality—these consequences of Puritanism make their appearance in the works of many writers such as Hawthorne, Longfellow, Emerson. Puritanism in America was indeed many-sided, and in the crucial formative years of the first generation, John Cotton took many important parts in the drama of Puritanism. Since no extended investigation of his works exists, it is time that their literary importance and cultural significance were considered—and considered in their historical context.

American scholarship of the last thirty years—since Perry Miller's epoch-making *Orthodoxy in Massachusetts*—has brought us a greater understanding of Puritan culture. The lesson which Miller taught, and which most recent students of the period have learned, is that theology cannot be ignored if one is to understand Puritanism. I have tried to learn that lesson too, but I have also taken advantage of other fruits of modern scholarship. Because Cotton's writings are so little known, my chief effort has been to communicate some sense of what Cotton was up to in his sermons and in his Congregational and other writings.

Few of Cotton's writings are accessible today. In addition to the obstacles to understanding which are discussed in my first chapter, extant copies of Cotton's books are rare indeed. Only those which are part of the debate with Roger Williams and a few others have been reprinted since the time of their original publication; only one has been reprinted in this century. Since I address readers most of whom have read at best only a few snippets of Cotton's writings such as are found in anthologies, I have quoted from his works and described them at some length. One of the briefest and most important I offer almost complete

—Cotton's once popular but now scarce catechism, *Milk for Babes*. To provide some sense of his individuality, I have also quoted with some frequency from his two best-known contemporaries in the pulpit, Thomas Hooker and Thomas Shepard. All quotations are modernized.

Cotton's books cannot easily be placed in discrete categories according to subject matter, for many deal with several matters. In order not to violate the integrity of the works, I have tried to consider each one separately but have related each to others with which it has important relationships. I have treated the sermons together, and have grouped the discussion of works which are primarily theological—as I also have those on Congregationalism, theocracy, Puritanism, and the Williams controversy. Some works have had to be considered in more than one context, and most in the context of Cotton's career. For the reader who is interested in a fuller treatment of Cotton's life, Larzer Ziff's recent *The Career of John Cotton* is warmly recommended.

I am grateful to the Research Committee of Florida Presbyterian College for a generous grant which aided this study. The staff of my college library has been most helpful, especially Miss Mary Tillman, Mrs. Barbara Thomson, Mrs. Merle Doran, Mrs. Pauline Melcher, and Mr. William F. Harrison. Mrs. Lois Willhoite was a very helpful typist, and Professor Sylvia E. Bowman an admirable editor. For her encouragement and wise counsel, I am most grateful to my wife Katherine.

EVERETT H. EMERSON

Florida Presbyterian College

Contents

Chronology

1584 Birth of John Cotton, son of Roland Cotton, lawyer in Derby, England.

1593- Attended Derby Grammar School.
1597

1597 Matriculated as a sizar at Trinity College, Cambridge University.

1602 Commenced Bachelor of Arts.

1603 Made fellow of Emmanuel College, a Puritan institution.

1606 Commenced Master of Arts.

1608- Head lecturer, dean, and catechist, at various times, for
1612 Emmanuel College.

1609 Preached funeral sermon for Dr. Robert Some.

1609 Experienced religious conversion from preaching of Richard Sibbes.

1610 Ordained to the ministry.

circa
1611 Preached university sermon which converted John Preston.

1612 Chosen vicar of St. Botolph's Church, Boston, Lincolnshire, with 1500 communicants.

1613 Commenced Bachelor of Divinity.

1613ff. Taught Cambridge students who came to live with him.

1613 Married to Elizabeth Horrocks.

1615 Salary now one hundred pounds a year. First manifested non-conformism.

1615 Established Congregational system within the parish.

1621 St. Botolph's stained glass destroyed. Cotton examined by Bishop Monteigne.

1629   Helped make plans for Massachusetts Bay Colony.

1630   Preached sermon at Southampton to departing members of the Massachusetts Bay Colony.

1631   Elizabeth Horrocks Cotton died, childless.

1632   Married to Sarah Hawkridge Story, a widow with one daughter.

1632   In hiding to prevent being summoned to appear before Bishop Laud.

1633   Resigned in May from St. Botolph's vicarship.

1633   Cotton and his family left in June for America.

1633   First son, Seaborn, born on way to America. Cotton chosen teacher of Boston church in October.

1635   First daughter, Sarah, born.

1636   Appointed in May to committee to prepare a draft of laws for the colony.

1636- Roger Williams banished in winter.
1637

1637   September-October: synod condemned antinomianism.

1637   Cotton appointed in November to first Board of Overseers of Harvard College.

1637   Elizabeth Cotton born.

1638   Mrs. Hutchinson excommunicated in March.

1640   Publication of *The Whole Book of Psalmes*. John Cotton, Jr., born.

1642   Invited to Westminster Assembly. Mariah Cotton born; later married to Increase Mather and mother of Cotton Mather. Again appointed an overseer of Harvard.

1643   Served as joint moderator of conference condemning Presbyterianism. Rowland Cotton born.

1644   Publication of Cotton's *The Keyes of the Kingdom*. Publication of *Mr. Cottons Letter Examined* and *The Bloudy Tenent of Persecution*.

1646- Cambridge Synod.
1648

1647 Publication of Cotton's *The Bloudy Tenent Washed.*

1648 Cambridge Platform prepared.

1649 Death of daughter Sarah and son Rowland.

1651 Seaborn Cotton graduated from Harvard.

1652 Cotton died in December.

John Cotton

CHAPTER 1

Three Hundred Years Remote:
The Man and His Age

OF THE FIRST GENERATION of New England writers, John Cotton (1584-1652) is doubtless not the greatest. To whom that title belongs is a subject of debate. Perhaps Roger Williams, Cotton's opponent in debate, is the best; but he is also one of the worst. Some would name Thomas Hooker or William Bradford. But since none of these had any intention of creating belles-lettres and since their values and interests seem very remote today, to judge their works in terms of their literary powers is neither easy nor altogether profitable.

If we adopt as a criterion for importance the revelation which a writer's works provide of the times in which he lived, John Cotton's writings have singular importance. He touched in his approximately thirty-six works nearly every aspect of the life of his times. He was a religious teacher, a law-giver, a defender of New England ideals, and a historian. He played many roles, for he considered the life of his community as an organic whole. Though as a minister he differed from most of his colleagues on certain religious issues, the very differences help us to understand the concerns of the day.

One of the reasons that Cotton is useful for understanding the past is the very remoteness we have noted. He is a man of the past, a past which is little known. The functions of his position as "teacher," his close identification with his denomination, even his education mark him as a man separate from our time. To come to some understanding of Cotton the writer is to gain an insight into the American past.

Douglas Bush comments that "It is hardly possible to exaggerate the importance of the sermon in the seventeenth-century world."[1] This observation suggests how distant we are from Cotton's time. Cotton was a preacher, and many considered him the greatest in New England. Cotton Mather quoted John Cotton's colleague in the ministry at his church in Boston as saying of him: "Mr. Cotton preaches with such authority, demonstration, and life that, methinks, when he preaches out of any prophet or apostle I hear not him; I hear that very prophet and apostle. Yea, I hear the Lord Jesus Christ speaking in my heart" (*Magnalia Christi Americana* [1702], III, 25-26).

Cotton's sermons constitute nineteen volumes of his published works, though some volumes contain only a single sermon. Some are topical, dealing with events of international importance. Most combine scriptural commentary with exhortations, warnings, and consolations; but even these often reveal a sense of time and place. All reveal a man of mildness and seeming simplicity, unless the subject at hand is the Book of Revelation or one which permits Cotton to reveal his rabid anti-Catholicism.

Before he came to America at the age of forty-nine, Cotton was identified with the greatest Puritan preachers of his day. He had heard William Perkins preach at Cambridge, where Richard Sibbes's sermons later converted Cotton. He had studied with Laurence Chaderton. He had written a prefatory epistle for an important collection of Arthur Hildersam's sermons. He was himself responsible for the conversion of the great John Preston. He sought counsel from John Dod. He was a friend of Thomas Goodwin. Samuel Clarke saw to it that Norton's life of Cotton was reprinted in 1662 in *A Collection of the Lives of Ten Eminent Divines;* here he was listed with more of the great ones, among them William Gouge, Thomas Gataker, and Robert Harris. But this whole world of English Puritanism seems very remote indeed, for with the coming of the Great Rebellion, it was transmuted and transformed, and soon modern secularism began its triumphs.[2]

Most modern readers of Cotton have expressed great disappointment with his sermons. The father of modern studies of colonial American literature, Moses Coit Tyler, finds no real merit in them. A more recent student of early American sermons, Babette Levy, rates them much below those of Thomas Hooker and Thomas Shepard. Their reactions have been typical. It remained for Larzer Ziff, Cotton's recent biographer, to see that precisely *because* Cotton is "immured in the seventeenth century" his works "offer us meaningful contact with the shaping past." To study Cotton is to understand the past; his sermons have a "conscious appropriateness to the moment in history."[3]

The easiest way to read Cotton's works is the wrong way. Perry Miller reminds us "of what is hard for most Americans, especially for the children of Puritans, to believe: the Puritans came to Massachusetts Bay not so much to found the United States of America as to execute a flank attack on the Anglican hierarchy."[4] The attack failed—if it can be said to have ever been executed—and the failure came at precisely the time that the New England Way was beginning to falter in Massachusetts. Americans prefer success stories, and it is more pleasant to imagine the Congregationalism which Cotton defended as the beginning of the American democratic tradition than as a scheme that had to be scrapped because it was unworkable.

Seven of Cotton's works are expositions or defenses of the New England Way, which Cotton was the first to call Congregationalism. More than his sermons, or more at least than most of them, these works provide an insight into the nature of his American experience. Cotton and many of his fellow colonists, as Miller suggests, considered their venture a great witness both to England and to the rest of the world they knew. Though he settled in Massachusetts, Cotton hoped through the force of example and through the persuasiveness of his pen to be able to return in triumph to his country, where Congregationalism would be established. The adaptations of Cotton's Congregationalism which took place after 1646 make Cotton's *Way of the Churches of Christ in New England* (1645) and *The Keyes of the Kingdom of Heaven* (1644) seem even to modern American Congregationalists mere historical curiosities unless the historical context is recognized. It is ironic that most of their few admirers see in them the beginnings of traditions which Cotton heartily hated.

One of the reasons for Cotton's eminence was his great learning. He was one of two New Englanders of the first generation to hold the Bachelor of Divinity degree, which required seven years of study beyond the Master of Arts, which was at that time achieved after three years of residence beyond the Bachelor of Arts. The very quality of this education suggests how much Cotton's world differs from our own.

At Cambridge Cotton studied logic, rhetoric, ethics, theology, Latin, Greek, Hebrew, some history, and some Aristotelian physics. The logic was that of Peter Ramus, sixteenth-century French Protestant, who tried to understand concepts by dividing them into dichotomies. Every subject could be subjected to the Ramist discipline, and the consequence was a great affection for method, for systematization. Logic, the tool of argument, went hand in hand with rhetoric, whose aim was elegance. The two were skills necessary for the public disputation which played a most important part in the academic program.

The ethics taught at Cambridge in Cotton's day was largely Aristotelian, with Aristotle's concept of the golden mean adopted as Christian good, and excess or deficiency identified as evil. With some inconsistency, the theological system which accompanied this ethics was Calvinistic. The *Institutes* of Calvin had replaced the works of the Scholastics, and nearly all English theologians were Calvinists from the 1560's until at least about 1620. Since the post-baccalaureate program was almost entirely a program for those intending to serve the church, theology loomed very large indeed. Cotton's writings show an extensive familiarity with Calvin and his followers Junius, Beza, Piscator, Zanchius, and Martyr; with Cotton's arch-opponent the Roman Catholic Bellarmine; with the Church Fathers, especially Augustine; with English theologians such as Perkins, Ames, Whitaker, Jewel, Cartwright, and Whitgift; and with the Scholastics, including Thomas Aquinas.

Latin was the necessary tool for all scholars, but Greek and Hebrew were even more important, as the languages of Scripture. Cotton's knowledge of Hebrew was examined when he was a candidate for a fellowship of Emmanuel College, Cambridge. Norton, Cotton's early biographer, tells us that his examiner chose Isaiah 3, "which hath more hard words in it than any place in the Bible within so short a compass." Cotton did well indeed; "such was his dexterity as made those difficult words facile and rendered him a prompt respondent."[5]

John Cotton—preacher, Congregationalist, scholar—is a man whose remoteness in time is less great than his remoteness in spirit. If we can avoid the danger of present-mindedness, we can learn much about our past from Cotton.

CHAPTER 2

Pleader for Purity:
The Puritan Writings

JOHN COTTON was a Puritan. This word has so many possible meanings that some effort at definition is obligatory. New England Puritanism developed when English Puritanism was permitted to be itself, cut off largely from forces unsympathetic to it. This New England Puritanism was in part what John Cotton made it, and Cotton was nearly fifty when he left England for America. For an understanding of Cotton's Puritanism, a knowledge of that of old England is vital.

English Puritanism was an effort to continue and complete the reformation of the Church of England, a project begun under Henry VIII. The uncertain path which the Church took after it separated from Roman Catholicism in 1534 became straighter when Elizabeth I ascended the throne in 1558. The path was thenceforth a middle way between the Protestantism of Calvin and traditional Catholicism. Its theology was Protestant, but it retained many of the traditional church practices and the episcopal hierarchy. Those who wished to eliminate from the Church whatever the "best Reformed churches" of the Continent had abandoned were called Puritans.

Initially, the Puritans wanted to eliminate such customs as the observance of saints' days, making the sign of the cross in baptism, the wearing of the surplice by the minister, and kneeling to receive Communion. When Elizabeth I made clear that there would be no further changes but enforced conformity to the middle way through the power of the bishops, some Puritans decided that the whole episcopal establishment should give way and that the Church government too should be purified. They favored Presbyterianism. The bulk of the Puritans would have been satisfied with lesser changes, but no definite Puritan program was ever decided upon. Puritan hopes for better days ran high at the accession of King James in 1603, but soon he made clear that he favored only minor changes. One consequence was the withdrawal of a few Puritans from the Church of England to establish separate congregations, but the bulk of the Puritans did not leave the Church.

Cotton's university was Cambridge, where Thomas Cartwright had preached Presbyterianism in 1569. His undergraduate college was Trinity, where the influential Puritan John Udall had studied in the 1580's. But probably Cotton came under far stricter Puritan influences when in 1602 he became a fellow of Emmanuel College. Here the headmaster was Laurence Chaderton, one of the most persuasive of Puritans, and a Puritan representative at the Hampton Court Conference with King James in 1604. In the Chapel at Emmanuel a non-Prayer Book service was followed, and ministers did not wear the surplice. Holy Communion was celebrated with the receivers sitting around a table. Cotton's wholehearted acceptance of the Emmanuel practices is suggested by the fact that he served as dean, catechist, and lecturer.

In 1612 Cotton was called to be vicar of the beautiful church of St. Botolph's in Boston, Lincolnshire, some seventy-five miles from Cambridge. Here non-conformity had been the rule for nearly thirty years. Cotton's predecessor as vicar had been found guilty of omitting the sign of the cross in baptism and of not wearing the surplice.

I Some Treasure

Despite his identification with Puritanism at Cambridge, Cotton conformed to the Church's requirements during his early years at Boston. But after about three years he decided that he could conform no longer. He therefore wrote out a defense of his new position, and he apparently circulated the document among his sympathizers. Years later, in 1660, when once again those who considered traditional ceremonies anathema needed to present their case, Cotton's statements were published along with a work by another author as *Some Treasure Fetched out of Rubbish: or Three short but seasonable Treatises (found in an heap of scattered Papers)*.

The first of the treasures is an answer to the question: Is it lawful for church governors to command indifferent things in the administration of God's worship? Must ministers use practices which Scripture neither requires nor forbids? Cotton's answer is of course, *No*. His very thoroughly Puritan view of the matter is that church governors can give orders concerning what is necessary and decent, and advise concerning what is expedient and decent; but they are not to command the indifferent and decent because to do so is to exceed the bounds of the authority given by the apostles, and to limit Christian liberty. To command the indifferent but decent is sin; to obey such commands is sin.

Cotton's second treatise in *Some Treasure Fetched out of Rubbish* is "An Inquiry Whether the Church May Not, in the Celebration of the Sacrament, Use Other Rites Significative than Those Expressed in the Scripture, or Add to Them of her Own Authority?" Again the answer is, *No*. The light of nature gives man some information concerning God and morality, but men "are utterly ignorant how or by what means God will be served, what He will bless for the instruction of His people" (28).

All Anglicans accepted the Church's position that "Holy Scripture containeth all things necessary to salvation," as the Thirty-Nine Articles put it; but Cotton and the Puritans contended that Holy Scripture provides a rule for worship as well as one of faith. "As in matters of faith," wrote Cotton, "so in matters of ceremonies significative pertaining to the worship of God: an argument doth hold from the negative, to disallow what is not found in the Scriptures expressly or by good consequence" (17).

This argument had been set forth by Thomas Cartwright in the 1570's; the classic answer was Richard Hooker's *Of the Laws of Ecclesiastical Polity*. The essence of Hooker's reply is this: ". . . those things that so belong to the way of salvation as to alter them is no otherwise to change that way than a path is changed by altering only the uppermost face thereof . . . in such things because discretion may teach the Church what is convenient, we hold not the Church further tied herein unto Scripture than that against Scripture nothing be admitted in the Church, lest that path which ought always to be kept even, do thereby come to be overgrown with brambles and thorns" (Bk. III, chap. iii, pt. 3).

Cotton's reasoning on the function of Scripture is based on Old Testament rules and practices. God commanded Israel to follow the ceremonial law to the letter. Moses did not dare to alter it. How can Christians dare to modify what God has commanded? "Both the Jewish and Christian Church are tied to the direction of the Scriptures, without which they might not presume to do anything in these matters" (12). The Christian is free from Jewish ceremonies, but he is not free to invent new ones. Here and elsewhere Cotton considers the whole law of God to be summed up in the Ten Commandments. Whatever is "commanded or forbidden is to be referred to some one or more of these Ten Commandments, though it be not expressly mentioned in any one of them" (22). It is the second which forbids man's inventions in God's worship, according to Cotton.

The difference between Richard Hooker and such Puritans as Cotton is in the understanding of man. Cotton is most suspicious of what Hooker calls discretion: ". . . the Scripture testifieth that every man is brutish by his own knowledge, nor more able to discern what in this case is fit and acceptable than a blind man is to judge of colors" (28). According to Cotton, "Man is carnal, blind, and impotent, and yet a lover of his own devices (no less than Pygmalion of his own picture)" (9).

Although the treatises in *Some Treasure,* which set forth his objections to Anglican ways of worship, have little originality, they are valuable for the clarity with which they exemplify the usual Puritan critique. Particularly clear is the resentment which Puritans felt at being unable to identify themselves with their Protestant brethren on the Continent because they were tied to the ceremonial of the *Via Media.* "The Scripture is the sole and sufficient rule of all immediate worship, internal or external, moral or ceremonial, as it is evident by the whole tenor of God's Word and the general confession of all Protestant divines" (34).

The Puritan insistence that "the Scripture is the sole and sufficient rule" has as its foundation the distrust of reason, which we have already noted; but perhaps just as important was the hatred of Roman Catholic ceremonial, which by Cotton's day was identified with attacks from abroad (the Armada) and treason at home. (To do what the Pope's Bull against Elizabeth I encouraged Catholics to do was declared treason in 1571, and in

1605 the Catholic Guy Fawkes had tried to blow up King, Lords, and Commons.) The "remnants of Romanism" in the Anglican Church led Cotton to argue that Christians were faced with an either/or decision, with no place for the Middle Way of Hooker. "Admit reason for an umpire in this matter [of how God is to be worshipped]" declares Cotton, "and images cannot be kept out of the Church, for no means is more profitable to inform the mind, confirm the memory, and move the affection than is the sight of a picture artificially made, cut or carved" (29).

From about 1625 increasing pressure was exerted by the bishops to put down the Puritans. A favorite device of congregations favoring Puritanism had been the hiring of a lecturer who did not have to participate in the ceremonial of the Church but who could provide proper Puritan sermons; now Laud silenced these lecturers. The increasing popularity of Puritanism led to still sterner measures against non-conformists. Those who fled to New England left because they knew that henceforth they had no opportunity to preach in England.

II Of Set Forms of Prayer

Cotton's self-exile finally permitted him to worship God in what he conceived to be the pure fashion described by Holy Scripture. In the New World Cotton did not, however, abandon his interest in the Church of England. He defended his own practice and showed, as did others in the New World, his continuing interest in purifying the Church of England. In a letter written on December 3, 1634, to a Puritan minister who had remained in England, perhaps John Davenport, Cotton offers three reasons for his leaving England. (1) Both Cotton and Thomas Hooker found that God had "shut a door against both of us from ministering to Him and His people in our wonted congregations. . . ."[1] (2) Though he had been willing to go to prison, he had been urged to minister to those of his Lincolnshire parish who had gone to New England. (3) They had satisfied their souls' needs by a mere matter of "two months' travel" and now they have no further need to fight against ceremonies. (Cotton has nothing to say here about the desirability of practicing Congregationalism, a reason he gave in 1648 in a preface to a book by John Norton.) Puritan ministers who remain in England can continue the fight against corruption in the Church of England, he suggests, through the purity of their "own outward practice," through their counsels to their people, and by "contending for the truth," even before magistrates (*Chronicles,* ed. Young, 439-43).

When in the late 1630's the desired further reformation seemed at hand, Cotton resumed his defense of the Second Commandment. About 1637 John Ball had sent Cotton a criticism of the New England opinion that written prayers were unlawful in church services. His work was published in 1640 as *A Friendly Triall of the Grounds Tending to Separation.* It asserted that a prayer is godly if its manner is holy and its matter fit, and if it deals with the needs of the supplicant. Cotton replied, according to Winthrop's *Journal* (I, 279), in 1638.

This time he attacked not "rites significative" but the use of written prayers—except for the Lord's Prayer and the Psalms, both scriptural. The attack, in reality a defense of the rejection of written prayers by the Bay Colony's churches, is a ninety-page treatise entitled *A Modest and Cleare Answer to Mr. Balls Discourse of set formes of Prayer* (1642). It does not seem modest to the modern reader, for Cotton argues that, once his reader has seen his arguments, for him to persist in his errors by continuing to use written prayers is a sin against his conscience. Such creations of man's imagination are sins against the Second Commandment, for ". . . God doth not ordinarily delight to bless the heart with gracious affections when the eyes go a-whoring after the imaginations and inventions of men" (7). As in the earlier *Some Treasure Fetched out of Rubbish,* Cotton looks to the Scripture to provide the precedent for church usage. To argue that the prayers of the Book of Common Prayer are expedient is to presume that "there is some help or means of God's worship expedient to the edification of the church, which never came into the hearts of Christ and His apostles to commend unto the church" (2-3).

One of the reasons for Cotton's rejection of written prayers is that their use implies a form of church government other than Congregational. It is unlawful "to worship God in a form of words devised by the officers of one congregation and prescribed and imposed upon others" (13).

In this work we reach an ultimate Puritan position. God demands even that men abandon the exclusive use of their own or other written prayers in their private worship.

III   Singing of Psalms

Akin to his work on prayer is the treatise which Cotton wrote with Thomas Shepard, *Singing of Psalmes a Gospel-Ordinance* (1650), presumably written some years earlier (Shepard, a minister in nearby Cambridge, had died in 1649). The legitimacy of singing in churches only songs recorded in the Bible is of course the position which Cotton and Shepard argue for, but some exceptions are permitted. On occasions of public thanksgiving a member of a church with musical talent may sing in church a psalm he has composed; those approving it may say "amen" to it. All are to join together in singing, even women and non-members of the church. It might be wise to line out the psalm—that is, to have someone say a line or two ahead so that those without books or unable to read may join in the singing.

Musical instruments are forbidden in the church, since they are not mentioned in the New Testament; but for private singing of spiritual songs, musical accompaniment is permitted. Since the original Hebrew melodies are lost, men may invent tunes and devise meters for the psalms. Surprisingly, those preparing the musical versions are cautioned to express not only the sense but also the art of the original.

Cotton and Shepard's work reveals a good deal of knowledge of poetry but less of music. Cotton's hand is especially prominent in the discussion of the musical practices of the church during its first three centuries.

IV   *Preface to* The Whole Book of Psalms

Closely related to *Singing of Psalms* is the preface to the *Bay Psalm Book*, or, as it is more properly called, *The Whole Booke of Psalms Faithfully Translated into English Metre* (1640). Zoltan Haraszti has demonstrated Cotton's authorship of this preface, or at least a draft of it still extant, which Haraszti published in 1956 in *The Enigma of the Bay Psalm Book* (107-15).

Cotton's preface appears to have been revised, perhaps by another hand, before publication.

The preface deals with many of the questions discussed in *Singing of Psalms*. Cotton makes plain that he favors congregational singing as opposed to singing by a choir: "If God had ordered choristers in the New Testament as He did in the Old, distinct from the body of the people, He would doubtless have given order and direction in the Gospel for their qualification, election, maintenance, etc., as He did for the musicians of the Temple" (*The Enigma*, 110).

The translation of the Psalms to be sung should be, according to Cotton, "into such verses as all our English songs run in (according to the poetry of our country)." The tunes themselves may be in the English fashion since "God hath hid from us the Hebrew temple tunes lest we should think ourselves bound to imitate them" (114). Haraszti assigns to Cotton the authorship of the translation of Psalm xxiii, but his case is not a very convincing one.

V   The Grounds and Ends of the Baptism

Although to some contemporaries the Puritans seemed to be thoroughgoing radicals, and the Congregationalists to be the most radical of all, John Cotton thought of the New England Way as the straight and narrow path of truth between the corruptions of Roman Catholicism and episcopacy on the one hand and the intemperance, heresy, and enthusiasm of the Anabaptists and Brownists on the other. From the days of Luther the arch-heretics had been the Anabaptists. A work which illustrates Cotton's opposition to the new revolutionaries is *The Grounds and Ends of the Baptisme of the Children of the Faithful*, published in 1647. Cotton's prefatory letter tells us, however, that the work was written several years earlier.

A son of a member of his old church, St. Botolph's, withheld his child from baptism after reading works against infant baptism. One of these the man brought to Cotton with a request that he answer it. Because he was otherwise occupied, he handed it on to Benjamin Woodbridge, then a young scholar living with Cotton, and asked him to prepare an answer. What Woodbridge prepared was unsatisfactory, for it was too "full of scholarship and terms of art." Cotton thereupon tried his hand at a less formal approach, and several years later he decided it was worth publication, despite its style.

The Baptists were subject to attack from the New England Congregationalists because they were Separatists; their practice of rebaptism indicated that they did not consider the Church of England an adequate source of things necessary for salvation. Separatists were considered seditious and schismatic; and, since their dissatisfaction with the Church caused them to be identified, in the minds of some, with the Puritans, it was important for the Puritans to dissociate themselves from the Baptists. In addition, the Baptists, who tended to be drawn from the lower class, had democratic predispositions.

The dialogue form had long been a popular means of propagandizing the Puritan point of view. It had been used by Anthony Gilby, John Udall, and Arthur Dent, all influential writers. But the sense of personality and the dramatic confrontation which enliven the dialogues of these writers is quite missing in Cotton's conversation between Silvanus (Cotton) and Sylvestre (a man attracted to Baptist tenets).

Cotton looks at baptism in the light of the covenant theory. Baptism is the New Testament means by which children come to be admitted to fellowship in the Covenant of Grace, just as circumcision was the Old Testament initiatory rite. Those within the Covenant who deny baptism to their children break, therefore, the covenant between God and man; they keep from their children the benefits of federal grace, which purifies the flesh and helps prevent one from lapsing back into natural depravity.

This concept of the Covenant leads Cotton into a kind of anti-Calvinist voluntarism (the doctrine that those offered grace may accept or refuse it). This teaching had been made popular by the influential Puritan John Preston. Cotton teaches that children of the Covenant are either the elect of God who will absolutely be given grace, or the non-elect to whom "He offereth to work the same in His own time, if neither their parents nor themselves reject or neglect the means which God offereth them" (20). This teaching is consistent with what Cotton taught around 1618 in his treatise on predestination, and again in the sermons of *A Treatise of the Covenant of Grace*. This voluntarism is in clear opposition to Cotton's usual strict Calvinism, but he seems unaware of the inconsistency.

It is strange that in permitting this book to be published Cotton should have left untouched his defense of the Anglican ministry. He denies that ministers' activities are ineffective because the bishops have usurped church powers; episcopacy had been abolished in 1643, four years before the treatise was published. He adds that ministers and people should try to overcome such usurpation, but they can if need be "avoid it by seeking the liberty of their consciences and of their churches in some sovereign countries or plantations" (182).

One of the ironies of history is that Puritanism was at its purest when it was most frustrated. In England the decay of Puritanism as a great moral and social force began with its triumph in the 1640's. In America Puritan organicism (the concept that church, state and society are one), though more attractive than it has appeared to some historians, was soon a highly conservative force. It embalmed the cultural life of New England pretty effectively until the days of its rebirth—the era of Hawthorne and Emerson, both products as well as critics of Puritanism.

CHAPTER 3

The Means of Grace:
The English Sermons

FROM ITS BEGINNINGS in the Elizabethan era, Puritanism had emphasized the importance of preaching. If the Catholic tradition puts its emphasis on the sacraments and makes the altar the focal point in the church, the Protestant tradition puts its emphasis on the sermon and makes the pulpit the focal point. Puritanism protested against the incomplete reformation of the Church of England, the *Via Media*; and, from the beginning, much of the protest was directed against the inadequacy of the preaching found in the churches. In 1559 Queen Elizabeth I admitted that very few ministers were preachers; she commanded the rest to read each Sunday one of the twelve homilies which had been first published in 1547. Though later supplemented by another collection of twenty, this was poor fare indeed. The homilies deal with such proper Protestant subjects as salvation by faith, the perils of idolatry, the excess of apparel, and the need to keep busy; but none of them is an exposition of Scripture. The Puritans looked to the instructions given by Saint Paul in II Timothy 4:2, "Preach the Word."

Another favorite Puritan text was Romans 10:17, "Faith cometh by hearing." Reading the Scripture or hearing a homily would not suffice; salvation required hearing sermons by a godly preacher. William Haller observes that "English Puritanism, denied opportunity to reform the established church, wreaked its energy during a half century and more upon preaching. . . ."[1] Puritan ministers were preeminently preachers, and their preaching was of many different varieties—as many varieties as preachers. All Puritan preachers believed it was necessary to

preach both Law and Gospel, but some inevitably found them-
selves more insistent on God's justice and some on God's mercy.
Some stressed God's love; some dwelt on what God demanded.
Most, of course, stressed both.

A good example of a preacher who emphasized the Law is
Thomas Hooker, Cotton's fellow emigré to America. In *The
Application of Redemption: The Ninth and Tenth Books* (1656)
Hooker demands the most complete penitence and humility of
his hearers if they would be saved. He warns them:

> Hear and fear then, all you stout-hearted, stubborn and re-
> bellious creatures, whose consciences can evidence that the day
> is yet to dawn, the hour yet to come, that ever you found your
> sins a pressure to you. They have been your pastime and de-
> light in which you have pleased yourselves, so far from being
> troubled for your evils that it is your only trouble you may not
> commit them with content, and without control. You are troubled
> with admonitions, and counsels, and commands, and threatenings
> that cross you in your sins. You were never broken hearted here
> for your abominations. Know assuredly that you will burn for
> them one day. Your proud hearts were never abased and laid in
> the dust. The Lord will ruinate both you and them. Never
> expect a good look from God. Set your heart at rest for that (11).

Quite different is the preaching found in many sermons of the
popular Richard Sibbes. In his *Bruised Reed and Smoking Flax*,
which went through at least seven editions, Sibbes warns against
preachers' demanding too much of men: "The ambassadors of
so gentle a Savior should not be over masterly."[2] Sibbes can
preach as gently as this: "We have a mighty deliverer. He loves
His children in the midst of all their deformities. Like a good
father, He tenders us in our weaknesses of soul and body, and,
as a father, pities His child the more for being sick. . . . He is
able to help . . . in all estates; His grace is sufficient; He hath
present help. What needs the child be dismayed for pain, when
the Father can remove it at His pleasure" (*Works*, VII, 99).

Even when his task is to warn his hearers of God's wrath, he
seems hardly to raise his voice. "Little do we know what times
may befall us. There is much danger abroad, and, we have cause
to fear, not far from us. It may be the clouds even now hang
over our heads. Oh, if we would be hid in the day of the Lord's
wrath, and have no evil come nigh our dwellings, let us, above

all things in the world, make sure our interest in Christ and title to the promise. We should seek to know God more, and then we would trust Him more" (*Works*, I, 425).

Though the style of all Puritan preachers is usually characterized as plain, many Puritans from Henry Smith (1557-1591) to Robert Harris (1578-1658) were witty, though much simpler and stylistically less elegant than many of their non-Puritan brethren. Commenting on Genesis 9:22 (Noah in his drunkenness), Smith observes: "It is said that drunken porters keep open gates. So when Noah was drunken, he set all open. As wine went in, so wit went out. As wit went out, so his clothes came off. Thus Adam, which began the world at first, was made naked with sin (Genesis 3), and Noah, which began the world again, is made naked with sin, to show that sin is no shrouder but a stripper. This is one fruit of the vine more than Noah looked for."[3]

Sibbes's style lacks this ostentation; it is always directed to one purpose: "When the love of God in Christ and the benefits by Christ are laid open in preaching of the Gospel to us, God gives His Holy Spirit, the Spirit of Christ" (*Works*, I, 23-24). Thomas Adams (c.1580-1660) sets forth the proposition in more theological terms: "Such is the infallibility of God's decrees and the inseparable effects that follow His heavenly intentions that the means shall easily perform the office they were sent to do: the preaching of the Gospel shall save those whom God hath determined to save by it."[4]

As a Puritan clergyman Cotton naturally made his reputation by his preaching. In fact through his sermons Cotton made two reputations: one for his manner, one for his matter. The first he made in 1609 when he was a fellow of Emmanuel College, Cambridge. Though the college was already famous for its Puritanism and though Cotton identified himself with the Puritan point of view, he seems to have thought of himself primarily as a scholar. As such, probably the best way in which he could display his learning was through the pulpit. A climax came when he delivered a funeral sermon for the late master of Peterhouse, Robert Some. Though neither this sermon nor any other early sermons by Cotton are extant, reports such as those of his biographer John Norton make it clear that Cotton was a witty, elegant preacher in a learned style—of the sort best known today from the sermons of Lancelot Andrewes and John Donne. Because of his learning Cotton developed a large following.

But he did not yet consider himself to be converted, and the preacher who spoke most to him, Richard Sibbes, was a plain preacher. Through the sermons of this man Cotton found himself in 1612 called by God's grace to salvation. But when it was his responsibility to preach again publicly, he found himself in a dilemma. Thomas Allen tells the story as he heard it from Cotton himself, much later:

> He, being according to his course to preach before the University and scholars in Cambridge, had a great conflict in himself about the composing of his sermon, *viz.* whether after the plain and profitable way, by raising of doctrines, with propounding the reasons and uses of the same, or after the mode of the University at that time, which was to stuff and fill their sermons with as much quotation and citing of authors as might possibly be. On the one side 'twas suggested to him that if he should not go the former way, he should not be faithful to the Lord in seeking His glory, but his own &c. And on the other side, if he should not show his learning, it would not only be a disparagement unto himself but also unto the College . . . (Prefatory epistle in Cotton's *An Exposition upon The Thirteenth Chapter of the Revelation*, 1655).

Cotton chose the plain and profitable way, much to the disappointment of some of his hearers; but, to his surprise, it was responsible for the conversion of John Preston. Then a fellow of Queen's College, Preston was to become master of Emmanuel and the most influential Puritan of his day, till struck down prematurely in 1628. With this evidence of the power of the plain style, Cotton adopted it permanently. He is said to have used Richard Sibbes's preaching as a model, and indeed the characteristics we have noted in Sibbes's sermons are to be found in Cotton's.

During his years at Boston in Lincolnshire and in Massachusetts Cotton preached thousands of sermons. John Norton tells us that in Cotton's English days he preached on Thursdays and Fridays in the early morning, on Saturday afternoons, and of course on Sundays. "Sometimes he was five or six hours in prayer and opening of the Word, so undefatigable in the Lord's work . . .", Norton reports.[5] In new Boston, Cotton preached

sermons on all of the Old Testament through Isaiah 30, on all
of the New Testament once, and on nearly all of it a second
time. On lecture days he covered many books of both the Old
and New Testaments again. His published sermons are not
necessarily his best or even representative ones; in most cases
they are reconstructions from notes taken by hearers. Some were
published without Cotton's consent, many posthumously. Some
volumes are expository sermons which treat a book of the Bible,
such as the Song of Solomon or Ecclesiastes. Some have a theme,
such as conversion and its consequences, which ties the series
together though the texts are from various parts of Scripture.
We have fourteen volumes in all, a total of nearly three thousand
pages.

Cotton devoted twelve hours of each day to study, but in
his sermons he makes few references except to the Bible. He
explained something of his view in a letter prefixed to Arthur
Hildersam's *Lectures upon the Fourth of John* (1629):

> When scholars furnish themselves with store of other writers,
> besides the Scriptures, and being little conversant in the
> Scriptures . . . their divinity proveth but humanity, and their
> ministry speaketh to the brain, but not to the conscience of the
> hearer. But he that diggeth all the treasures of his knowledge
> and the ground of religion out of the Scriptures, and maketh
> use of other authors, not for ostentation of himself, nor for the
> ground of his faith, nor for the principal ornament of his
> ministry, but for the better searching out of the deep wisdom
> of the Scriptures, such an one believeth what he teacheth, not
> by an human credulity from his author, but by a divine faith
> from the Word, and because he believeth, he therefore
> speaketh, and speaking from faith in his own heart, he speaketh
> more powerfully unto the begetting and strengthening of faith
> in the hearer.

I God's Mercy Mixed with His Justice

Frequently Cotton seems to have found a new theme or the
beginning of a new biblical book a source of inspiration. He
begins with vigor and freshness. Toward the end of nearly every
volume, however, he becomes increasingly prolix and repetitious.
An exception is the one volume of sermons which do not constitute a series, *Gods Mercie Mixed with his Iustice* (1641).

Though more uniformly interesting than most of the others, these sermons, which were delivered in England, are identical in form with the others. Let us consider the structure of the first sermon in *Gods Mercie*.

The text is Revelation 3:20: "Behold, I stand at the door and knock. If any man hear my voice and open the door, I will come in to him, and will sup with him, and he with me." This text Cotton divides into two parts: *behold*, which he calls a note of attention and admiration, and then the matter to be attended to. The latter he divides into three parts, each containing what he calls a double act: God's standing and His knocking; man's hearing and his opening; and God's entering and His eating. From this verse he then draws three doctrines: "The heart of man is the door of the soul"; "The patience and bounty of God is great towards sinners, even admirable great in calling them home to Himself"; and "Such as do hear the voice and knocks of Christ and do open the door of their hearts to Him, He will vouchsafe fellowship with them, familiar and continual fellowship with them, feasting of them and be feasted by them." Cotton thus is thoroughly methodical in his logical analysis of the text, but he is less careful in distinguishing the persons of the Trinity. Here, as elsewhere, "God" is presumably the Father; but here as elsewhere the Father and the Son are treated almost interchangeably.

Next, each of the doctrines is explained, partly by referring to parallel ideas and images found elsewhere in Scripture, partly by showing in detail what the words of the doctrine mean. For example, Cotton explains that God's patience (referred to in the second doctrine) is manifested in His restraint in punishing the sinner, in His issuing warnings before He punishes, in His delaying after issuing warnings, and in His restraint even in punishing.

Next come the reasons for the doctrine: *why* the heart is called the door, *why* God is so patient. (Four reasons are provided for God's patience, but none is given for the third doctrine.) Finally come the uses, or practical implications, of the doctrines. The doctrine that the heart of a man is the door of his soul shows that knowledge and wisdom count for nothing. If God is so patient, how ashamed should the man be who has not repented? If God grants fellowship to those who open their hearts to Him, what good reason there is to repent and accept God!

This plan of organization is not original with Cotton; it was used by nearly all Puritan preachers and by many who showed no dissatisfaction with the established Church. Most of the plan is outlined by the influential William Perkins in his *Prophetica* (1592); another Puritan, John Udall, contributed the idea of providing reasons for the doctrines.[6] The Puritan sermon organization was recommended by the official *Directory of the Publique Worship of God*, published in London in 1644. It was "found by experience to be very much blessed of God, and very helpful for the people's understanding and memories" (34). Many Puritan preachers put great stress on the uses of doctrine; Cotton seems to have been concerned with all of the parts equally; but in a given sermon he may choose to develop one aspect and to ignore another, as when he omits reasons for one of the doctrines.

Like others who used this sermon plan, Cotton addressed various kinds of people in his congregation in the *uses* sections of the sermon. In *Gods Mercie* he addresses uses to "all men of understanding," "every soul that knows his heart and life is unprofitable," "all the professors of the truth of Christ Jesus," those who do not know God, despairing sinners, and "God's servants." Sometimes the use is for consolation, sometimes for exhortation, or for admonition, or for trial. Only in some of the weekday lectures of the 1640's does Cotton not speak as an evangelist.

The listing of divisions and subdivisions of uses, reasons, doctrines sometimes makes Cotton's sermons appear not methodical but merely confusing. When the second part of the third part of a discussion has three parts, we may very well lose track of Cotton's argument. But these sermons were not meant to be read but heard with note-taking equipment in hand, and the scheme lent itself readily to note-taking. Heads of Puritan households were expected to examine their families on the contents of a sermon, a good reason for taking notes. The very existence of this volume and many others is due to the simple style and methodical plan; for Matthias Swallowe, author of the prefatory epistle for *Gods Mercie,* refers to the book as "some broken notes of his powerful soul-searching sermons taken from his mouth by the diligent hand of some well-disposed hearers and followers."

Cotton's adherence to the plain style did not prevent his developing biblical metaphor in a pleasing and interesting way. The second sermon in *Gods Mercie* has as its text this metaphorical description from Revelation 7:14, "These are they which came out of great tribulation, and have washed their robes and made them white in the blood of the Lamb." This passage inspired Cotton to produce these words:

> . . . poor men, yes, yet they were adorned with robes. Had it not been enough to say "washed their garments"? What, must poor men be set up with robes? Yet robes they have, and white robes, and they washed in the blood of the Lamb. So that it shows you that the servants of God that come well out of tribulations, they get more royal spirits than ever before, for robes become royal persons and princes. When robes in good earnest are put upon any, they put upon them princely majesty; a spirit of glory and royalty is put upon them. He carries himself no more like a base drudge of this world. He is able to overwrestle all tribulations and afflictions of this world . . . (39).

Gods Mercie is a good introduction to Cotton as a preacher because it shows us his concept of God. The title, presumably chosen by Matthias Swallowe, suggests that Cotton's God is both merciful and just; and, indeed, the sermons all suggest God's patience, mercy, concern, and restraint. Yet at the same time Cotton makes us very much aware of God's potential wrath:

> . . . where had Paul been if he had been struck to death as well as to the earth? He had never returned then to have seen the light of the living. God therefore . . . considers what sorry things we be, and that if He should but stir up His wrath, we should be utterly undone. He will therefore stay many years before He pour out all His wrath and utterly consume us (15).

> . . . .

> Make account there is no grace God hath given you, be it never so eminent, but God will take some time to prove you in it, and how you may employ it to the utmost good. God that gives talents will not have them put under a bushel; He will one time or other put you to express the utmost strength of your strongest grace, whether it be obedience, or faith, or patience, or meekness, or love, or zeal (104).

Cotton's God is, however, much more attractive, much less inclined to terrify a congregation than is the God of most of his contemporaries; and in this respect Sibbes's influence seems clear. Thomas Shepard, another Bay Colonist, argued in his English days in this fashion: "God shall set Himself like a consuming infinite fire against thee, and tread thee under His feet, who hast by sin trod Him and His glory under foot all thy life. A man may devise exquisite torments for another, and great power may make a little stick to lay on heavy strokes, but great power, stirred up to strike from great fury and wrath, makes the stroke deadly. I tell thee, all the wisdom of God shall then be set against thee to devise torments for thee."[7] In contrast Cotton's God is loving and tender indeed.

II   A Brief Exposition of Canticles *(1642)*

Much of *Gods Mercie* remains interesting; it is probably as attractive as any volume of sermons we have from Cotton. The volume is brief (135 pages) and is available in a modern facsimile edition. But other volumes of Cotton sermons have their interest too, and, though it is not fashionable to admire a work because of its quaintness and antiquarian interest, Cotton's *A Brief Exposition Of the whole Book of Canticles* (1642) does have such an appeal. (I use the edition of London, 1648.) The sermons which constitute the volume date from Cotton's English ministry. The exegesis was notable in its day, and the subject was considered a fascinating one. After Cotton's death a second series of his sermons on the same text, delivered in America, was published. In the later volume, prepared by Cotton, he tells us that the 1642 volume was published "without my privity."

The poetry of the Song of Solomon has of course made it for all ages a very attractive book; Christians have frequently read it as an allegory of Christ and the church. Cotton reads it as a history of the church from Solomon's time to Judgment Day—in other words, as a prophetic book. He is aware that the Song of Solomon is regarded by some as sensuous, but he reproves such an attitude. He rejects the ancient synagogue law prohibiting men under thirty from reading the book—for Cotton believes that it can only fire young men with heavenly love; to him it is "a divine abridgment of the acts and monuments of the church" (9).

Reading the book as history was not original with Cotton. The practice goes back to the Talmud, and the Targum goes into considerable detail in its allegorical interpretation. Adopted by the Christian church, the allegorical reading was not seriously questioned until the time of Erasmus. Cotton follows Thomas Brightman's interpretations to some extent, but is mainly original.

The history which the book describes will seem to most readers somewhat less clear than Cotton found it. He finds, for example, prophecy in the ninth verse of the first chapter: "I have compared thee, O my love, to a company of horses in Pharaoh's chariots." Here we have, says Cotton, a description of the condition of the church of Judah after Rehoboam fell away so that God sent Shishak of Egypt to subdue Judah. To support this view, Cotton reminds his audience that Shishak caused kings to draw his chariots like horses.

Presumably one of the reasons that Cotton was unhappy to see his own book in print after he had left England for America was that he was embarrassed by his interpretation of the fifth verse of the first chapter: "I am black but comely." This verse is useful, declares Cotton, because it teaches "the children of the Church not to separate from the Church for corruption's sake . . . but to see her comeliness also" (30-31). He further comments, "It was a sin in them to be angry with the Church as some of the separatists are, and do depart from us. . . . What and if some cast off England? Shall we reject it because some of the sons of her mother do?" (31-32).

Cotton shows his Congregational tendencies by his definition of the church as "an assembly of many good Christians or saints . . . set in order . . . amongst whom Christ walketh, they enjoying fellowship with Him in His public ordinances, and He with them" (180). "Such churches," Cotton explains, "and congregations are queens whom the ministers and congregations do with mutual free consent choose either the other; as when the people do give up themselves first to the Lord and then to the ministers by the will of God. Of this sort are sundry congregations in England, and very many in the Reformed sovereign churches. Other congregations which have ministers thrust upon them without their liking and consent, and whom ministers have to them by some clandestine conveyances, are more like to concubines" (185).

While in England, Cotton thus clearly adumbrated his later views, though of course he was less strict in his requirements for a true church. Unlike most Puritans who thought of the Christian church in England in terms of the national Church of England, Cotton considered the church to exist in terms of the particular, visible church. A church must have five conditions, Cotton taught in this work: free acceptance and maintenance of the minister by the people, powerful preaching, discipline (specifically excommunication), and the discovery of saints through preaching.

The collection of sermons in *A Brief Exposition of Canticles* is marked by many observations of interest to the student of Cotton, but since in a later volume on the same book of Scripture Cotton provided a fuller and more mature treatment of the subject and a better text, we leave this book—which amounts to a collection of notes—after this slight consideration.

III   The Way of Life

The longest of Cotton's sermon volumes is *The way of Life. Or Gods Way and Course, in bringing the soule into; keeping it in, and carrying it on, in the wayes of life and peace* (1641). This too, according to the prefatory epistle, was published without Cotton's knowledge. The sermons were delivered in England, as a passage on page 389 indicates. In this passage Cotton complains of those who "come to offer their children in baptism; they never consider what they have in hand; come only to take the rites of the Church and what the laws of the kingdom require; put God off with mere compliments. . . ." Such a situation Cotton never permitted in America.

This volume resembles many Puritan treatises on conversion, for example, those of Cotton's American colleagues Thomas Hooker and Thomas Shepard. Like their accounts, much of Cotton's is ostensibly an objective description of the salvation process, as the title suggests. *The way of Life* is in reality a series of sermons intended to be the means of salvation; for, as the fourteenth chapter of the Westminster Confession puts it, ". . . the grace of faith, whereby the elect are enabled to believe to the saving of their souls, is the work of the Spirit of Christ in their hearts and is ordinarily wrought by the ministry of the Word. . . ." Or, as Cotton declares in this volume, God gives grace to those who seek it, especially to those who seek it in sermons. "If God give thee but an heart to feel thine own want . . . He will give you a Spirit of grace" (12).

One knows that God has given him grace, according to Cotton, when he recognizes his own sinfulness and loathes himself. He recognizes, too, the deadly forces which surround him: the flesh, his own doubts, his coldness of heart, his pride and wrath; and from these he seeks relief from God through prayer. He prays for a soft and believing heart, a humble spirit, and sanctifying grace. This eagerness to pray and the ability to do so are God's gifts of grace.

As Cotton proceeds, the method becomes clearer. How does one know if he is saved? By seeing whether he can do what the preacher says can be done only with God's grace. This approach neatly reconciles a willingness to acknowledge the salvation process as God's work with the practical fact that the minister must urge his hearers to act. Cotton's description of the second effect of God's saving grace also demonstrates this reconciliation. Through grace, says Cotton, God gives man power to see that he has crucified Christ and to recognize that through the crucifixion there is redemption for man.

The subsequent effects of saving grace which Cotton describes are sufficiently unnatural to relieve Cotton of the charge of preaching "boot-straps theology" pure and simple. He who receives God's grace, says Cotton, sorrows for sin so much that he can be said to go into a mourning greater than that appropriate for the loss of an only child. "The spirit of grace helping us to mourn, it will make our grief to grow, to be more at the last than at the first. . . . It lasts while life lasts" (54).

Perhaps because he recognized that he was making it sound very difficult to be saved, Cotton describes the times as a period when God was giving His grace with peculiar abundance—and to the worst of men. Thus Cotton tried to appeal to all of his hearers, especially those far from God, to seek humiliation. The reward for true humiliation is assurance of salvation: "Dost thou find thy will and inclination to [sin] die and decay in thee so as that thou hast no desire or delight in sin? The liveliest spirit thou hast to this or that sin is now evaporated and wasted, and thy heart is furnished with graces opposite to those sins? . . . If it be thus with thee, then surely God hath pierced thy heart, and thou art in an estate of salvation" (130).

Though much of Cotton's preaching is evangelistic and addressed therefore to the sinner whom he would save by encouraging penitence, Cotton speaks also to those who have previously felt themselves called. If God does not speak to a man's sins in a sermon, says Cotton, he is like a child not remembered in his father's will. By such means Cotton brings home to his audience that they are in the presence of the means of grace when they are hearing a sermon.

Cotton brightens up his discourse by comparing the means of grace, the sermon, to a sword. "The sword of God, take it as it lies in the Word, and it is like a sword in the scabbard, and the exposition is but the brandishing of it; but when application is made, that thou art the man that has done this, not to endure this is an argument of a carnal heart, though sometimes even God's own people do not love to be particularized" (171-72). This last phrase suggests the gentleness and tender-mindedness found throughout most of these sermons. But in the sermons on Acts 2:37 he resolves to be firm. He preaches on contrition, which is necessary since "The very first work of living and saving grace gives a deadly stroke to the life of sinful nature" (125). Perhaps this is his strongest passage:

> A direction and advertisement to such as yet find their hearts whole and unbroken: take heed how you content yourselves in such a condition. Consider what our Savior said to Saul, "It is hard to kick against the pricks"; to dash the naked soul against the curse and wrath of God is an hard business . . . but many a man that goes on in sin saith he feels no such hard work in sin. But thou wilt feel at the last that it hath been but dashing against pricks, and if not in this world, then with more horror in another. You little know what anguish of soul for sin means. Can you provoke God to anger and not yourselves to confusion?
>
> (132-33)

At his toughest Cotton remains gentle indeed; he can scarcely be said to have put the wrath of God before his hearers.

Cotton's mildness is even more striking when one turns to Thomas Hooker's sermons on the same text in the ninth and

tenth books of *The Application of Redemption.* Here Hooker
suggests that God is sometimes merciful to sinners and might
be merciful to some of the sinners present. Then he exclaims:
"Oh, is it not pity to cast such dainties before dogs, and pearls
before swine? Did I say it was possible? True, I said so, indeed,
but it's pity thou wert in the hearing of it. It's pity to speak such
precious encouragements to such poisonous and malignant spirits
that will pervert all to their own ruin. The word is past and
cannot be recalled, but take these preservatives, or corrosives,
rather, to eat out that impudent corruption" (28).

At times Cotton reveals, unwittingly, the difficulty of reconciling the theory that conversion is God's work with the need
to be exhortatory in preaching. He argues, against the semi-
Pelagian Roman Catholic position, that experience proves the
Calvinists are right in teaching that God's grace is irresistible:
"The people of God can tell [that] when God first looked into
their hearts they were most drowsy at such a sermon, and their
hearts more wandering that day than ordinary, and so unfit for
mercy in themselves" (182). But Cotton would not have those
who have not yet been called sit and drowse through *his*
sermons. He asks his hearers to reflect: "Have I lived here in a
congregation where I have been followed with means of grace
almost these eighty years, and know not to this day in what
estate my poor soul stands before God? Now take it to heart, and
see how you will answer this to God. Never rest and sleep in
such a condition lest in the end you be past remedy" (184).

Another seeming inconsistency in Cotton's preaching is that
he speaks of the need of the preacher to be specific, to point
to man's sins and name them; yet he is thoroughly vague. For
example in part of this collection of sermons, in the 226-page
"The Life of Faith," Cotton frequently refers to "a Christian
holy life." The content of this life is never specifically described;
the phrase seems to mean going to church diligently, attending
to the sacraments and the sermon, reading the Bible, and for-
saking one's (unspecified) lusts.

Students of economic history such as Tawney have frequently
remarked that Puritanism encouraged capitalism. One of the
men who by Cotton's own testimony taught him much, Paul
Baynes, had this to say about the relationship of prosperity and

goodness: ". . . observe that the next [nearest] way for a man to thrive in his outward state is first to grow rich in his spiritual. . . . God doth undertake to keep damage from his, while they are occupied in his service."[8] One can see that Cotton's teachings, too, might encourage a spirit of individual enterprise. According to Cotton, a Christian may be

> busy in his calling from sun rising to sun setting, and may by God's providence fill both his hand and head with business, yet a living Christian when he lives a most busy life in this world . . . he lives not a worldly life (270).

> . . . .

> That God may be glorified in Jesus Christ, this is the sum of his eating and drinking and buying and selling &c.; this is the upshot of all; this is all for Christ . . . (271-72).

> . . . .

> The more God blesseth a man with a fair estate, the more doth faith quicken him to fear and serve God and enlarges him thereunto (457).

Diligence in one's vocation is so supremely important for Cotton that he conceives of it as the outward parallel to the inward life of faith, the life of prayer and thankfulness, and the hearing of sermons. "As soon as ever a man begins to look towards God and the ways of His grace, he will not rest till he find out some warrantable calling and employment. . . . A Christian would no sooner have his sin pardoned than his estate to be settled in some good calling" (437).

Though Cotton connects diligence in one's vocation with Christian responsibility, and though he is painfully vague of most of man's other responsibilities, he makes clear that at the time he prepared these sermons he was no Antinomian. He always assumes here an intimate connection between faith and good works, between redemption and sanctification—the kind of relationship that later Anne Hutchinson called a Covenant of Works. Part of Cotton's "legal" preaching is his comment on Galatians 2:20, "I am crucified with Christ; nevertheless I live; yet not I, but Christ liveth in me; and the life which I now live in the flesh I live by the faith of the Son of God, Who loved me and gave Himself for me":

> There is no man who seeks righteousness by Christ but he destroys the body of sin; no man partakes in justification by Christ but he is crucified with Christ, and if we therefore be justified by faith in Christ Jesus, there is no man weaned from sin more than such men, no man more weaned from the things of this world, nor so much, as he that is justified by faith in Christ Jesus. No man hath fellowship with Christ in His death pardoning his sin but he hath fellowship with Him also purging him from sin . . . (262-63).

IV A Commentary on First John

The sermons in *The way of Life* are tied together by their theme; many are in fact on the same text. Much less unified is the volume of sermons entitled *A Practical Commentary or An Exposition with Observations, Reasons, and Uses upon The First Epistle Generall of John.* Though not published until 1656, this thick volume contains sermons evidently delivered in England, for on page 85 Cotton says, "Tell a child of some thing—let but his father say, he will buy him such a thing at London, or he hath it laid up for him, he rests well pleased." And on page 156 he speaks of "we in England." Also, the prefatory letter reports that an Essex minister had heard most of the sermons.

The variety of the subject matter of these sermons can only be suggested: the composition of the Bible, Roman Catholic traditions, the teachings of the Church Fathers, morality, history, and, most extensively, fellowship with God. Unlike many of Cotton's sermons, these display somewhat ostentatiously their author's extensive reading. He repeats the Schoolmen's reasons why Christ did not become an angel to save the fallen angels. He considers what the Father and the Son did in the period before the world was created, five thousand years before. He criticizes the Fathers because they did not know Hebrew. He discusses the religious significance of lots:

> . . . all lots are religious, whether they be about holy things, as choosing apostles, or civil, as casting lots about division of lands, or any other thing, to determine controversy or the like, as they cast lots for Christ's garments, for it is not the object

that makes a thing lawful or unlawful, as whether we swear in
religious or civil matters, or lusory [gaming], because whatsoever we swear about, we call God to be a witness, so in all kinds
of lottery, whatsoever it be about, we appeal to God, who is
disposer of all things (Proverbs xvi.33), for man being but
causa per accidens of the event of the lot, there must be some
cause *per se*, and that is God, for whatsoever it be about, though
matters of pastime or lusory, it is a religious ordinance because
it appeals to divine providence, and therefore is to be avoided
(127).

The subject of lots interested the Puritans; Thomas Gataker, a
contemporary of Cotton, wrote an entire treatise on the subject.

Once again it is interesting to note Cotton's early views on the
Church and Congregationalism. He defends the reading of
prayers and the Church of England, but he admits that the
Church has weaknesses. They are not failures in fundamental
doctrine but only in "the skirts and some circumstances" (157).
The chief problem is the relationship of minister and people.
Cotton protests that even this difficulty is not universal: "many
of us are elected by the people's approbation, or by such as
are set up by the king and state, and if God bless our ministry
to convert thousands to God by that means, it is an evident sign
God approves our calling, for if it were anti-Christian they would
not convert souls to God" (157). Here Cotton seems to speak
against the Separatists again.

In this volume Cotton once again gives great emphasis to the
role of good works. He teaches emphatically that good works do
not justify a man, yet by them "we know that we are justified."
"If a man walks in a constant course of obedience to God's commandments, he may thereby know that he is in Christ, and this
must needs be an encouragement to works" (72). Cotton comes
as close in this instance as anywhere to preaching a doctrine
of salvation by works.

More orthodox is his gloss on I John 2:2, "And He is the
propitiation for our sins, and not for ours only, but also for the
sins of the whole world." Cotton comments: "Jesus Christ is
the propitiation for the sins not only of believing Jews but likewise of believing Christians all the world over." Here is the pure
High Calvinist doctrine of the limited atonement.

In this volume of sermons from time to time appear passages

which are so laced with biblical citations as to make the work almost unreadable. Thus Cotton comments that the Incarnation was "the manifestation of Him [Christ] to the inward man; for though they knew Him to be God (Psalm cx.1), mark our Savior's urging that place (Matthew xxii.44, 45) and man (Genesis iii.15) to be of His Church, the King (Psalm ii.8, 9), the Priest (Psalm cx.4, Daniel ix.17), the Prophet (Deuteronomy xviii.18, Job iv.25)" (13). This practice of citing is rather too common, and it keeps the work from having any literary value.

V   Christ the Fountain of Life

Closely related to this *Commentary* are the sixteen sermons which make up *Christ The Fountaine of Life: or, Sundry Choyce Sermons on part of the fift Chapter of the first Epistle of St. John.* The reason that Cotton could lavish so much attention on just six verses when he had devoted the makings of a book of sermons to the whole five chapters of I John appears to be that the sermons of *Christ The Fountaine* were lecture-day addresses, and on these days he chose to focus on a theme with which his text dealt instead of offering, as he did on Sundays, a full commentary on his text.

Cotton explains that St. John's identification of Christ with life means that without Christ man's sins merit death, that justification is the price of eternal life. The sanctified life, the effect of justification, is also to be understood as the life which is identified with Christ.

The specifically Puritan character of Cotton's work is manifested by the fact that ten of the sermons are devoted to this problem: How can one tell if he possesses Christ and thereby possesses life? The need for proof was central in the strict predestinarian atmosphere; fatalism would be the logical outcome of predestinarian teaching except for what Weber calls "the idea of proof." "Because of it the psychological result was precisely the opposite."[9] The strenuous efforts which Weber implies, by which one demonstrates that he is among the elect, are fully prescribed by Cotton. He who possesses Christ prizes Him above all else and abases himself. He desires to know Him and His power to be gracious. He is affected by Christ at the heart, the will, and the affections. He does Christ's will. He respects every commandment of God as a means of honoring and worshiping Christ.

Then one notes a subtle shift in Cotton's point of view. In the second sermon he describes not so much how one knows whether he possesses Christ but how to possess Him. Although several ways are suggested, Cotton of course leaves in each case some initiative to God. If emphasis on proof, however, encourages human efforts, it is fair to say that Cotton teaches in this sermon something very close to voluntarism. He argues, for example, that when God

> sees men are willing to forgo their most darling, delightful sins, willing to break off all impediments that stand between God and them, the soul of God is grieved in such a case, and it pities Him now that such a soul should be without Him; and then it will not be long ere God stirs up means of deliverance, and He Himself will reveal Himself unto them. . . . God is then abundantly ready to pardon, when men forsake their own ways and thoughts, and throw away the sins that hang about them (20).

> . . . .

> when we come to God, and desire Him not only to take them [our sins] from us but begin to consider our own ways and iniquities and to put them from us, out of our hearts and hands . . . then the Lord presently gives us the Lord Jesus Christ, and life and healing in Him . . . (21).

Although much has sometimes been made of the covenant concept as a crucial part of the salvation process in Puritan preaching, Cotton describes it as merely one of the several ways by which man may come to possess Christ, and it is as demanding a way as any. In fact, Cotton almost makes the covenant a Covenant of Works rather than of faith, for the terms of the covenant include promising to do God's will and sacrificing one's self—one's soul and one's body. It differs from what Cotton elsewhere calls the Covenant of Works only in that one who breaks the covenant finds that God is willing to reseal it after confession and repentance.

Perhaps the most troublesome inconsistency in Cotton's preaching is that he recommends steps which he says will prepare a man for salvation while elsewhere he teaches that performing these same steps is a sign that one is already saved. In the third sermon of *Christ The Fountaine* Cotton teaches that Christ *will* enter one's heart if one prepares the way for Him by humility, by loving Christ, by being willing to do whatever Christ would have one to do, by believing that there is hope for him, by casting out all lusts. In the eighth sermon he teaches that to go willingly to Christian duties argues that one is of the elect. And in the later *Treatise of the Covenant of Grace* (1659) he teaches that the whole process of salvation, even the preparatory steps, is God's work and not man's, and that "any saving preparation in the heart" is a sign of election (39-40).

One can only fall back on the Reformed concept of the sermon as an explanation of this inconsistency. Heinrich Heppe offers a sophisticated explanation, but it is one to which Cotton would doubtless have subscribed.

> . . . the Holy Spirit so works upon man as to esteem him a personal creature and so does not regard him as a clod or a stone, but acts so that enlightened by the Word and impelled by grace man receives in conversion the will to convert to God and so his conversion takes the form of spontaneity. Yet since in conversion every sort of cooperation of man's will with the Holy Spirit is completely excluded, the activity therein exercised by the Holy Spirit is no merely natural, merely moral or mediate activity (no mere *suasio per verbum*), but at the same time and pre-eminently an immediate, supernatural one, in which the Holy Spirit avails itself of the Word as its means, yet, in a way completely independent of the natural activity of the Word, works essentially and irresistibly . . . upon the thought, will, and life of man.[10]

Cotton puts the matter somewhat similarly in *Christ The Fountaine* when he defends exhortation of the unconverted: "for though in nature we are neither willing nor able to look after Christ, but look at Him as a vain refuse commodity . . . God many times conveys such a Spirit of grace into us as gives us power to receive Christ . . ." (173). He argues that ". . . no saving gift of God can be wrought in the heart without faith, and . . . faith comes . . . by hearing . . ." (181).

The difference between John Cotton and other preachers of his tradition is that Cotton is more cautious. He does not promise his hearers that if they prepare for the coming of Christ, He will come and save them, as does Thomas Hooker:

> You see the means that God appointed for the conveyance of grace and mercy to you, nay, that Christ Himself may take possession of you, and it is the way and means that never will deceive you. Would you have Christ to dwell in you? Then be humbled and be not wanting to yourselves, and then Christ will never be wanting to you. Labor to get this humiliation, and Christ will come immediately into your souls. Have a heart but rightly disposed, and without all question Christ will come to comfort and refresh thee upon all occasions (*The Soules Implantation* [1637], 108).

We have seen how demanding a preacher Hooker was; perhaps he thought that by demanding much he could promise much. Cotton asked less and promised less:

> . . . this is the preparation we must make for Christ to come unto us. You have sometimes heard this fully spoken to, that is, when the high mountains of our great spirits and lofty looks are brought so low that we are content to be nothing in our own eyes, that we have all we have in Christ, and are able to bring nothing to Him, and are willing that He should do with us what is good in His own eyes; then these high mountains being brought low, we are made fit for Christ to come in to 'us . . . (41).

John Calvin himself is less demanding than Cotton, and he promises quite as much as Hooker:

> . . . when we shall be well persuaded that it is to those who are most miserable that He addresses the salvation which He acquired, provided they recognize themselves as such, and they humble themselves, and they are entirely confounded, rendering themselves blameworthy (as they are) before the judgment of God; that is how we shall have easy access to be sharers of the righteousness which is offered to us, and by which we obtain grace and favor before God.[11]

Christ The Fountaine of Life once again demonstrates Cotton's inability to sustain his interest or at least the interest of his readers throughout the series. But even late in the volume we find an occasional attractive passage, such as this one, which compares Christ to an elder brother:

> As if an elder brother should set a child, one of his younger brethren, to get his father a posey of flowers, and the child out of ignorance should gather some weeds and put [them] in it, and the elder brother gathers out the weeds and sprinkles the flowers and then presents them in the child's name to the father; so doth Christ to us, while we gather up petitions here and there, and, as we think, for the best, and some truth and work of grace there is in them, yet some weeds of sinful folly, then Christ takes them out of our hands and pulls out the weeds and sprinkles them with the blood of His cross . . . (223-24).

VI   God's Promise to His Plantation

Doubtless the most interesting of Cotton's English sermons is *Gods Promise to his Plantation. . . . As it was delivered in a Sermon* (1630; I use the edition of 1634). The carefully chosen text was II Samuel 7:10: "Moreover I will appoint a place for my people Israel, and I will plant them that they may dwell in a place of their own and move no more"; for the occasion was the departure of John Winthrop and four hundred others on the *Arabella,* bound for Massachusetts from Southampton.

After an explanation of the historical situation in II Samuel, Cotton explains how God makes room for a people by casting out the people's enemies by war, or by arranging for them to be given a portion by courtesy, or by emptying a land of its inhabitants so that it is vacant. It is the religious responsibility of colonists to live in the land appointed them by God.

Cotton then describes six circumstances in which it is proper for a people to emigrate—all six presumably relevant for the colonists. They may move to gain knowledge; to conduct merchandising; "to plant a colony, that is, a company that agree together to remove out of their own country, and settle a city or commonwealth elsewhere" (9); to employ their talents better; to obtain "the liberty of the ordinances" as in the days of Queen Mary or "when some grievous sins overspread a country that threaten desolation" (9-10); to take advantage of a special providence "if sovereign authority command and encourage such plantations by giving way to subjects to transplant themselves and set up a new commonwealth" (11).

The most interesting part of the sermon is the advice which Cotton offers to the new colonists. Of course Cotton emphasizes the importance of church "ordinances": preaching, discipline, and the sacraments. But he warns them also: "Be not unmindful of our Jerusalem at home, whether you leave us, or stay at home with us" (18). He asks that the colonists care for their children, who in a new land might well become degenerate. But it is the possibility that the colonists might become effective missionaries that captures Cotton's imagination: "Offend not the poor natives, but as you partake in their land, so make them partakers of your precious faith. As you reap their temporals, so seed them with your spirituals. Win them to the love of Christ, for whom Christ died. They never yet refused the Gospel, and therefore more hope they will now receive it. Who knoweth whether God have reared this whole plantation for such an end" (19-20). Cotton's hopes for the Indians were not of course realized. Later, when he became the great apologist for the colony, he was particularly sensitive to the failure of the Indian missionary effort, and he therefore magnified John Eliot's few successes as much as possible.

A reader of Cotton's English sermons may very well be curious to see what changes took place in his sermon technique and his approach with a different audience and a different setting. But we should remember that he was almost fifty when he left England for America; his patterns and methods were well established.

CHAPTER 4

Champion of the Way:
The Congregational Writings

JOHN COTTON'S most important task was that of spokesman for the new form of church government which developed in Massachusetts Bay. Although scholars differ on the historical background of American Congregationalism, they do agree that the adoption of this church polity was of particular importance and had very significant consequences.

Congregationalism in time was responsible for the development of a sense of spiritual separation from England quite as great as the physical separation, and this sense did much to give New England its peculiar moral strictness and its occasional provinciality. Yet the Massachusetts Bay colonists had no intention of cutting themselves off from England. They were English, and they looked to England not with sentimental nostalgia but with genuine concern. Many thought of America as only a temporary haven, and a goodly number of colonists did in fact return to old England when the Church of England lost its episcopal hierarchy.

The founders of the Massachusetts Bay Colony intended, as John Winthrop said on the voyage to America, "by a mutual consent through a special overruling providence and a more than ordinary approbation of the churches of Christ to seek out a place of cohabitation and consortship under a due form of government both civil and ecclesiastical." Because they were a select company, selected by God, and because they were entering a new land, they could be in a unique sense what God intended them to be. The Bay Colonists thought of themselves as "a city upon a hill; the eyes of all people are upon us."[1]

The essence of the due form of ecclesiastical government which they adopted, Congregationalism, is what Winthrop called "a mutual consent," the idea of the covenant. A Congregational church consists of a covenanting group of believers who acknowledge their faith to one another. Such a covenant was adopted by a group within Cotton's Lincolnshire church, so that Congregationalism existed within the episcopal system. This scheme of things was not intended by Cotton and the other covenanters to be a separation from the Church of England, for Separatism was schism and radicalism. It meant a break with the past as fundamental as had been the separation from Rome; and, since Cotton and most other Puritans believed that grace had come to them through the ministry of the Anglican Church, to separate from it seemed blasphemous. Separation had serious practical disadvantages as well. But when these non-Separatist Puritans came to America, they did in fact separate themselves from the Church of England, its government, and its system of ordaining ministers; but the descendants of the Puritans down into the eighteenth century denied that they had done so.[2]

I *The Background of Cotton's Defenses*

Cotton's writings about Congregationalism must be considered against the background of events in both Massachusetts and England. Cotton went to a Congregational colony; there he joined a church which had been "gathered," according to Congregational terminology, within a month of the arrival of its members. Cotton did not have his son, who was born at sea, baptized until he had himself joined a church "1. because they had no settled congregation [at sea]; 2. because a minister hath no power to give the seals but in his own congregation" (John Winthrop, *Journal* [1908], I, 107). These reasons suggest that, before he arrived, Cotton had a good knowledge of Congregational theory. American Congregationalism as it was to be formulated in the Cambridge Platform was to a considerable degree established before Cotton's arrival, and the theory Cotton had found in his reading of William Ames's works. Still, his acceptance of the already established system might in fact have been reluctant had he not feared a movement toward Separatism through the work of the extremist Roger Williams, who was demanding such a complete break with the past that members of Congregational churches would have been forbidden to hear sermons by those not Congregationalists.[3]

Cotton's dealings with Roger Williams in the next decade and his problems with Anne Hutchinson, both discussed elsewhere in this study, affected Cotton's career as a Congregationalist. Williams' banishment in the winter of 1635-36 led to the extensive debate between Williams and Cotton, and, in the course of it, Congregational Massachusetts was shown to be an enemy of toleration. A consequence of Williams' attack and of events in England was, as Raymond P. Stearns observes, that "Whereas in 1641 the Bible Commonwealth was looked upon as an experiment in ecclesiastical liberalism, by 1645 it had become a stronghold of conservatism."[4] Cotton's part in the Anne Hutchinson episode became grounds for attacks on his orthodoxy, and arguments *ad hominem* became part of the attack on Congregationalism.

Four years after Cotton left England, events began to happen which did much to isolate the New Englanders from their old home, though at first the incidents appeared propitious. In 1637, the efforts of Charles I and Archbishop Laud to force a Book of Common Prayer on the Scottish Church resulted in the expensive Bishops' Wars and in a need on the part of Charles for additional funds. When Charles, seeking funds, called a parliament, it was more interested in airing grievances which had accumulated since the previous parliament, eleven long years before. Charles soon dissolved it. Convocation, meeting simultaneously, intensified the current bad feelings by promulgating seventeen new canons, nearly all offensive to the Puritans.

The year 1641 saw another parliament called to raise funds for the needy Charles. But, instead, the Long Parliament voted to impeach the Puritans' chief opponent in the Church of England, Archbishop Laud, and it also considered eliminating episcopacy from the Church. Those who most resented episcopacy were parish ministers, who wanted for themselves the powers which the bishops were enjoying. Spokesmen for a change, including John Milton, quickly explained the need for the elimination of the prelates and for the substitution of presbyteries. When the Parliament ordered the establishment of the Westminster Assembly, a mammoth committee of English divines and Scottish commissioners was appointed to look into the matter; and the hope was that soon a substitute for episcopacy would be established. The problem facing the ministers at Westminster has been brilliantly diagnosed by William Haller:

> The majority of the divines in the assembly, under the urging of the Scots, were proposing that the disciplinary power of the church and the all-important authority to ordain ministers and license preachers be vested in the presbytery or "classis" made up of representatives from the various parishes of a given district. . . . But they were forgetting that they had risen to their present position through the opportunities formerly allowed them to enlist the support of converts and followers regardless of parish boundaries and independent of official central authority. Every Puritan group which at any time joined together to engage a lecturer tended to become a "gathered church" centered in its preaching minister and self-limited in membership to his convinced personal followers.[5]

With Charles engaged in fighting Parliament in the First Civil War, debate in the Assembly between Presbyterians and Congregationalists delayed a decision as to what polity would be recommended, though no decision could effectively be made until the issue of the war had been settled. Americans, including Cotton, entered the debate through their books to propose the establishment of the New England Way in England. But English Congregationalists sought toleration for themselves and then, to gain political supporters, toleration for others. Thereafter, the term "Independents" was used for the coalition of sects with which the Congregationalists had identified themselves. Now a conservative force, the Presbyterians strongly opposed the sects, for many of them had left orthodoxy, and vigorously attacked the Congregationalists for the encouragement of the schism they were providing.

Though the debate ended with the victory of the Presbyterians, it meant little, for the army opposing Charles had gained more and more political power, and it was identified with the Independents. Oliver Cromwell's soldiers saw the Congregational form of government as a means of freeing them from external religious restrictions. Now the Church of England was theoretically Presbyterian, but all other Protestant groups, save the episcopalians, were permitted to organize churches on a voluntary basis, and the Presbyterians lacked influence and—what they most desired—power to discipline.

Cotton's efforts to promote Congregationalism of the intolerant New England variety bore a poor harvest indeed. The few fruits were repulsive to him, and it was difficult for one in remote Massachusetts to understand what made Presbyterians so unhappy with Congregationalism. Cotton did come to recognize that, compared with the Independents, the Presbyterians might not be so evil after all; at least the Presbyterians had not embraced toleration. Perhaps Cotton was fortunate not to live until the chaos caused by the saints in arms led to the restoration of episcopacy in 1660.

II   The True Constitution

Back in 1633, when Cotton became teacher of the church of Boston, an observer with foresight might have predicted that a scholar like Cotton in a town with such great potential would be an important man in the colony. Within a year he had begun to draw up a defense of the Congregationalism established in Massachusetts Bay, but the time when it was needed to further the cause of Congregationalism in England did not come until 1642. Then it was published as *The True Constitution Of A particular visible Church, proved by Scripture.* No works describing the New England Way had been published before because of censorship and because it would not have been wise to advertise to the episcopal hierarchy the American practices. Now Cotton provided both description and defense, and, although he later prepared more detailed statements, this is an important one because of its early date. It went through four editions. (I use the third, published in 1644 as *The Doctrine of the Church, To which is committed the Keyes of the Kingdome of Heaven.*)

A church begins with Christians, Cotton teaches. The members of a church rightly organized are those called to salvation by God; they form a church by confessing their sins to each other, professing their faith, and binding themselves by a covenant. The members choose officers, consisting of a pastor, who exhorts the members and dispenses wisdom; a teacher, who dispenses knowledge; and ruling elders, who assist the pastor and the teacher by admitting new members, excommunicating those who should not be members, and seeing to it that "none in the church live either inordinately without a calling or idly in their calling" (3). They also prevent and heal offenses in morals and doctrine, prepare matters for congregational consideration, admonish, and visit the sick. Cotton cites Scripture to support all of this organizational plan.

The proper worship service in a Christian church consists of ten activities: (1) prayer, (2) singing of psalms, (3) reading of the Bible (the Word), (4) preaching the Word by giving the sense of it and applying it for the use of the congregation, (5) "where there be more prophets . . . they may prophesy [preach] two or three, if the time permit," (6) the asking of questions of the preachers (a privilege not available to women), (7) baptism of believers and their children, (8) the Lord's Supper, (9) taking the collection, and (10) the blessing.

All churches are equal and independent. If, however, a church offends in doctrine, other churches may admonish it to mend its ways. If the admonition is not heeded, other churches may condemn it and withdraw from fellowship.

Though historically important, this short, clear work has no literary pretensions, and it lacks a sense of the moment in history when it was written. It uses the simple question and answer form. It says nothing of the development of the system of Congregationalism.

III A Sermon Delivered at Salem, 1636

More important for students of Cotton and Congregationalism is *A Sermon . . . Deliver'd at Salem, 1636,* which finally found its way into print in Boston in 1713. The sermon itself is prefaced by a retraction in which Cotton tells how, while still in England, he had protested to the pastor of the Salem congregation when magistrates arriving in America were not permitted to receive communion or have a child baptized. "You went hence," Cotton had written, "of another judgment, and I am afraid your change hath sprung from New Plymouth men."[6] The influence of Plymouth on Massachusetts Bay Congregationalism through Deacon Fuller is still being debated. Cotton's own statement here suggests a strong influence, but later he emphasized the continuity of the Congregational tradition from the pre-emigration period.

Since he had made his complaint—Cotton in 1636 confessed—a diligent search of the Scriptures had shown him that he was wrong. He had learned that the covenant and its gifts, such as the sacraments, do not belong to all believers but only to those "confederate with Abraham." The Old Testament required that the faithful should join the family of Abraham. The Christian equivalent is joining a congregation. Cotton had learned too, he tells us, that a minister has no power unless he is called by a people; his power then is limited in that it extends only to those who have called him. Just as no one can be excommunicated but those who have been admitted to communion, so only those can be admitted to communion who are possible subjects of excommunication—that is, church members.

The sermon which follows this address explains in some detail the theology of the covenant, which, significantly, Cotton expounded at this time, just before the beginning of the Anne Hutchinson controversy. This theology, accepted by most Puritans whether or not they were Congregationalists, has been considered by some scholars as a factor which mitigated the arbitrariness of the Calvinist God and permitted preachers to teach that man has the power to do much toward his own salvation. In fact, this sermon teaches nothing like voluntarism.

Cotton, like other covenant theologians, conceives of two covenants: the Old, or the Covenant of Works; and the New, or the Covenant of Grace. The first of these God made with Abraham; by it He promised life to those who give exact obedience to His laws, statutes, and judgments. By it man agrees to be cursed of God if he breaks the covenant by violating the commandments. The second covenant was made "with the people of Israel and Judah . . . especially after their return from Babel and yet more especially under the days of the New Testament . . ." (8). By this covenant God promises His people Christ and everlasting communion with Him in return for faith in Christ, the obedience of faith (the righteousness such as only those given grace can have), and repentance. That this second covenant is a perpetual one, Cotton teaches, shows the necessity for a church covenant:

The use of this point . . . may show us . . . a ground of that which some of us (yet but few) saw the truth of, in our native country, namely the necessity of a church covenant to the institution of a church. "Come, and let us join ourselves to the Lord." That which doth make a people a joined people with God, that doth make a church. What is that? The Covenant of Grace doth make a people a joined people with God and therefore a church of God, and therefore you shall find that when the Lord establishes Israel for a church unto Himself, He maketh this covenant (21).

The covenant thus is a theological doctrine as well as an ecclesiastical one.

IV   *Letter to Lord Say and Seal*

In New England the covenant was political too. Since the requisite for membership in a church was faith, and since God gives sanctifying grace to those who have faith, the best rulers, according to Massachusetts thinking, ought then to be church members. To an English nobleman who contemplated settling in Massachusetts, Lord Say and Seal, this scheme did not look attractive. Cotton justified the Massachusetts policy in a letter written in 1636. It was not published until 1764, when it appeared in Thomas Hutchinson's *History of Massachusetts Bay.*

Cotton believed that, although the churches and the state should be intimately related, they should also be separate. The state should be organized according to the pattern which he believed God described in the Bible so that the churches may be vigorous. The state exists, in part, for the sake of the church. Though Cotton believed that God described the ideal political order, he thought that He left room for man's discretion. Democracy, often identified with Congregationalism in the history of ideas, was not, according to Cotton, an available option: "Democracy I do not conceive that ever God did ordain as a fit government either for church or commonwealth. If the people be governors, who shall be governed? As for monarchy and aristocracy, they are both of them clearly approved and directed in Scripture, yet so as referreth the sovereignty to Himself, and [God] setteth up theocracy in both as the best form of government in the commonwealth as well as in the church."[7] But theocracy did not mean that the ministers were to rule. God ruled, through His saints. The fact that church members chose the leaders, Cotton protested, did not mean that the form of government was democratic; for democracy is government by the people, not by the governors. It is right for the church to choose members as governors, for the church has the function in Massachusetts of preparing "fit instruments both to rule and to choose rulers."

The fact that the people, or rather those church members who chose the responsibility of serving as "freemen," were given political power was itself a consequence of covenant theory. Edmund S. Morgan notes in *The Puritan Dilemma* (90-96) that, according to Massachusetts Bay political theory, the government did not derive its power from the people, yet the establishment of government depended on a voluntary covenant made by the people. The officials who administered this government were chosen by the freemen but empowered by God. This covenant theory of government was part of the European movement which led to the conception of all social relationships as contractual ones.

A year after Cotton's correspondence with Lord Say and Seal another questioning letter arrived. This time thirteen English ministers wrote to the New England clergy to question them about their church practices. They were distressed at reports that the American churches held that a set form of prayer and the use of the liturgy were unlawful; that the Lord's Supper was forbidden to those not members of a Congregational church; that baptism was administered only to the children of church members; and that the chief power of the churches was in the hands of members. Cotton promised to send an explanation of the situation, and the following year he did present the defense of Massachusetts' rejection of set forms of prayer which has been discussed in an earlier chapter. No full answer to the other questions was sent till 1639, when John Davenport answered. Both the original letter and Davenport's reply were published in Simeon Ash and William Rathband's *A Letter of Many Ministers in Old England* (London, 1643); Cotton's letter is in the Cotton Papers in the Prince Collection of the Boston Public Library.

V   A Copy of a Letter

Several years before his extended defenses of the New England Way were published, another letter which Cotton wrote to a correspondent in England found its way into print. In this letter, published as *A Coppy of a Letter* (1641), Cotton assured his correspondent that prospective church members were not required to disclaim the churches of which they had formerly been members, nor to profess repentance for their former communion with English churches, and that they did not covenant never to have communion with the English churches. Cotton noted that the principal cause for excommunication from the Massachusetts churches had been the rejection of communion with the English churches. Such a rejection had been demanded by Roger Williams, who wanted the new churches to cut themselves off from what he considered to be the corruption of the English churches. It is interesting to note that a correspondent of Governor Winthrop wrote: "Your disclaiming of Mr. Williams' opinions and your dealings with him so as we hear you did took off much prejudice from you with us."[8] Cotton's disclaimer was published just two years before Williams began his attack on Cotton on the issue of toleration.

A Coppy of a Letter demonstrates the importance for the Bay Colonists of maintaining the fiction that their churches were part of the Church of England. Since the government of the colony was authorized by the English crown so that its power could be said to be legitimate, the colonists could, in Perry Miller's words, "call any church they established part of the Church of England, and, therefore, by grace of magistrates of their own creating, could enforce complete obedience to it." Thus they could "transport both the English state and Church to Massachusetts and there reform them at will" (*Orthodoxy in Massachusetts,* 100).

VI   The Way of the Churches

The full description of the New England Way which Cotton had promised was prepared in the early 1640's. Entitled *The Way of the Churches of Christ in New-England,* the work circulated in manuscript for some time, according to the prefatory epistle, which complains of the difficulty of obtaining the authorities' permission to have such Congregationalist works published. The authors of this prefatory epistle consider *The Way* as supplemental to *The Keyes of the Kingdom,* published the year before; but Cotton later complained that *The Way* should not have been published, as it represented a position which he no longer held. The variations from Cotton's position in the authoritative *Keyes* seem slight, but the chief one is the important question of the power of the elders, which—as we have seen—was considered to be crucial by the English Congregationalists. In *The Way* Cotton emphasizes somewhat less the power of the elders and somewhat more the power of the congregation. The work would thus have been less appealing to a power-seeking English clergyman. The Englishmen who published *The Way* considered it to contain basically their position, on the virtues of which, they believed, it shed new light. *The Keyes* had a peculiar importance because the New England Way was conceived in it as derived from authority; today *The Way* seems far more attractive and interesting.

The Way of the Churches, a work of twice the length of *The Keyes,* describes some of the theory of Congregationalism but is in the main a description of Congregational practice in New England. Cotton emphasizes the importance of religion in New England when he reports that those who go there and desire to join a church profess "that it was the principal end of their coming, to enjoy the presence of the Lord in the liberty and purity of His ordinances" (6). Sometimes newcomers come in a group, and the group (like Thomas Hooker's) is "loath to part company and yet so great that they cannot well join in any one church already established without too much impeachment of their outward estate and livelihood, the chiefest part of the lands belonging to each church being prepossessed by others before them. . . ." They then may decide to form a new church, in which case they "inquire out someone or other of eminent gifts, usually such as have been preachers of good esteem in England, who may guide and go along with them in so great an action . . ." (6-7).

In New England the next step is to tell the governor and some of the local magistrates of the intention to form a church, and to invite their representatives and those of nearby churches to meet with them on the day of the church-gathering. (In fact, the General Court in 1636 had ordered that no church was to be gathered without the prior consent of the majority of elders and magistrates of the Colony.) On that day a spokesman for the members of the church being gathered professes on their behalf repentance and faith, propounds the "covenant of promise," denies any ability in themselves to keep the covenant, and professes "their acceptance of the Lord for their God, and the Lord Jesus (the head and Savior of His church) to be their king, priest, and prophet, and give up themselves in professed subjection unto all His holy ordinances" (8).

Much of *The Way of the Churches* is devoted to a discussion of the proper officers of a church, their responsibilities, qualifications, and method of selection. A point of particular concern to Cotton is the role of the ruling elder as distinguished from the preaching elder. He is not a layman, Cotton insists, but is ordained and has important powers, particularly in connection with admission of new members and maintaining high moral standards in the community. (Ironically, the position of the ruling elder was abandoned after the first generation in New England.)

It is to the ruling elders that a candidate for church membership applies. They examine the applicant's knowledge of religious principles, his experience with grace, and his moral behavior ("his godly conversation among men"). If he is acceptable to the ruling elders, they tell the church. If the members believe him to be worthy, the applicant publicly confesses his sins, explains how God's grace drew him out of his sins and into fellowship with Christ, declares that he has "good knowledge of the principles of religion," professes his subjection to the Gospel and his desire to walk in it "with the fellowship of that church" (55). After testimonials are offered in his behalf, he accepts the church covenant and is a member.

It is unfortunate that Cotton did not describe the implications of "walking with the fellowship of a church." One of his parishioners, Robert Keayne, kept a notebook on the proceedings of Cotton's church; and the notebook, still extant, gives us a surprisingly attractive picture of the fellowship. On the basis of his study of the notebook, Larzer Ziff calls it "a deeply felt relationship" which gave a sense of social solidarity.[9]

The Way is an answer to Cotton's critics (unnamed) as well as a description of American practices. The description of how the churches admit members is followed by a defense of three Congregational practices: that only those possessing "gracious qualification" are admitted as members, that members are received by covenant, and that power is given to the people in the admission of members. The first practice, as we shall see, is defended at length elsewhere in Cotton's works; the second and third defenses reveal much about Cotton's habits of mind and predispositions.

Early in *The Way* Cotton upholds the covenant as an Old Testament institution and asserts that it is "evident by the light of nature that all civil relations are founded in covenant." Here he uses the same familiar arguments, adding that in the New Testament the church members at Ephesus are referred to as fellow citizens with the saints, and the word *citizens* implies a covenant since all civil citizenship is based on a covenantal relationship. Since Cotton elsewhere rejects the testimony of the light of nature in determining religious questions (it is man's vain imaginings), this argument is not very persuasive. The Old Testament argument is indeed consistent with Cotton's basic assumption that laws made in the Old Testament apply in New Testament times unless Christ specifically abrogated them. Still Cotton is uneasy about the lack of a clear description of a church covenant in the New Testament: ". . . in the days of the New Testament, the magistrates and princes of the earth being aliens and enemies to the church, the apostles thought it meet to speak of this covenant not plainly but as it were in parables and similitudes . . ." (62). It is his very reliance on the Bible for authority that makes Cotton unconvincing here. (An influential Congregationalist of a later generation, Solomon Stoddard, protested, "There is no syllable in the Word of God intimating any such thing" as a church covenant.[10]

Again when Cotton defends the Congregational practice of admitting new members by the consent of the old ones, he recognizes that it may sound dangerously like democracy for the people to have so much power; but he protests that he is compelled to accept the principle since Christ gave the power of the keys to the church. Were Cotton not so unsympathetic here with his own argument, he might be more effective in defending the covenant. As it is, he sounds like a defender of the standing order who is something of a trimmer.

More effective, but much less politic, is Cotton's explanation of why members of the Church of England are not permitted to receive the Lord's Supper in New England churches though members of other Congregational churches are admitted. The difficulty with the distinction is that it made clear the actual separation which existed between the Church of England and the American churches—a separation that Cotton and his colleagues were trying to deny. It is perhaps this portion of the book, as well as his discussion of the power of the church members, which made him regret the publication of the work.

Members from other New England churches are permitted to receive the Lord's Supper if they bring a letter of recommendation from the church of which they are members or if their churches have made known their desire to have their visiting members received. But those who are members of the Church of England and have left their home parish are not members of a particular church, nor do they bring letters of recommendation. In addition, they come from churches which are defiled with five public offenses, which they must first specifically repent: they have belonged to a national and therefore unscriptural church (earlier he denied this was a sin); they have come to the Lord's table without public profession of repentance and faith; they have come to the Lord's table with ignorant and scandalous persons; they have worshiped God with the inventions of men; and they have accepted an unscriptural form of church government. In *A Coppy of a Letter* (1641) Cotton had denied that new members were required to make such confessions.

As a whole, *The Way of the Churches* reveals Cotton as a confident proponent of Congregationalism, though he had difficulty with certain objections to it. He makes clear that he considers New England churches to be the model which English churches should follow, and his extensive criticisms of the most Puritanical of the English churches in the closing pages of the book demonstrate no awareness that New England Congregationalism was not to get far in England.

VII The Keys of the Kingdom of Heaven

In 1642, the year following the publication of *A Coppy of a Letter*, Lord Say and Seal, who had not after all emigrated, and several other members of Parliament wrote to Cotton as the leading Massachusetts Bay minister and also to Thomas Hooker and John Davenport, the leading ministers of Connecticut and New Haven, urging them to return to England, where they were needed as members of the Westminster Assembly. None of the three attended, but Cotton wrote a book to persuade the assembly to adopt for England the Congregational way. This work, *The Keyes Of the Kingdom of Heaven* (1644), was endorsed by the two leading members of Cotton's ecclesiastical party in England, Thomas Goodwin and Philip Nye. *The Keyes* was important because of its approach and because of England's high regard for Cotton. His opponent Thomas Edwards called him "the greatest divine," the "prime man of them all in New England."[11]

The Keyes would be more interesting if it were a description of what was going on in the Massachusetts churches instead of being a statement of Cotton's conception of the authority and power of the church as they are presented in Scripture. The book went through seven printings, which suggests that it was widely read. The moment has long since passed when the issue was a pressing one, but its historical importance is suggested by the fact that the leading English Presbyterians wrote books in answer.

The Keyes Of the Kingdom of Heaven is presented as an explanation of Matthew 16:19: "And I give unto thee the keys of the kingdom of heaven: and whatsoever thou shalt bind on earth shall be bound in heaven, and whatsoever thou shalt loose on earth shall be loosed in heaven." The keys were given, according to Cotton, not only to Peter, to whom Christ spoke, but to all the apostles, or rather to each of the apostles separately. The power which they received went in turn to all of the church. When a group of Christians gather together and form a church, they now possess as a church the power of the keys given to Peter and the apostles. Thus the basic unit of the Christian church is the individual congregation, and it is from this unit that all ecclesiastical power is derived. For example, "the complete integrity of a minister's calling" rests on the power given him by his people (37).

What is this power, the power of the keys? According to Cotton it is, first, faith, the faith common to all believers. Second, it is the power to enter the fellowship of a church, to choose gifted men as officers, to partake of the sacraments, and to censure offenders. The officers are given powers of various kinds by those who choose them. Elders have power to preach, to call the church together, to judge and pronounce sentences on offenders before the church, to separate the true disciples from the rest of the people if the latter fall away from Christ, and to perform certain other admonitory and administrative functions.

These are the basic powers given by Christ to His church, according to Cotton. There is no transcendent power given to an official such as a diocesan bishop. Beyond the individual congregation there is, however, the synod where elders may meet to treat three kinds of problems. First, the synod may help provide peace or light for a church that seeks it, as did the church at Antioch; second, it may reprove a church which is corrupt in doctrine, when private reproof has failed; third, it may try to effect a general reformation when the churches seem to be growing corrupt. The synods may not enjoin what is by nature indifferent (what Scripture neither requires nor forbids); they may not legislate but may see that the laws which Christ made are published and observed.

The power of the synod was the question that most separated Presbyterians and Congregationalists, but closely related to it was the relationship of the members of the separate churches to one another. Presumably because his English brethren had not looked with pleasure at the lack of friendly relationships among members of different congregations, in *The Keyes* Cotton modified the position he had set forth in the address which preceded his Salem sermon of 1636. He now taught that one of the liberties given by Christ was communion with other churches, not only through the synods which could be formed, but also by members of a church receiving the Lord's Supper in other churches. A church might work with other congregations by keeping an eye on visiting church members, by recommending a church member who moves to the neighborhood of another church, by giving and receiving supplies, and by propagating the faith through missionaries.

Cotton also defines the proper relationship of church and state. The church does not derive power from the state but is subject to it, for the state has power to enforce civil peace. Civil peace required "The establishment of pure religion in doctrine, worship, and government according to the Word of God, as also the reformation of all corruptions in any of these" (50).

As developed in practice, this arrangement did as much to prevent the spread of heresy and toleration as the discipline of Presbyterian synods could have done, but to Presbyterians it must have sounded like the despised Erastianism developing in England. In Massachusetts, magistrates claimed the jurisdiction over offenses against the first four of the Ten Commandments, and the General Court of Massachusetts drew up in time a code which required punishment by the state for such heresies as denying the resurrection of the body.

The Keyes Of the Kingdom is written in a most cautious, unpolemical tone. It was intended to serve the cause of moderation, or so at least said those who arranged its publication. The English Congregationalists in a preface to the book describe the New England Way as a middle way between Brownism or Separatism, which reduces the power of the elders by putting church government into the hands of the people, and Presbyterianism, which reduces the power of the individual elder in his church by putting church government into the hands of a district presbytery. For Cotton's English colleagues the publication of an American work such as *The Keyes* had two advantages over the publication of their own efforts, such as *An Apologeticall Narration*. First, it had experience behind it and therefore seemed more authoritative than their own pronouncements. Second, since it was not their own statement which they were issuing, they were less subject to attack for it by the Presbyterians.

VIII   The Way Cleared

Although Congregational theory dates from the early years of the seventeenth century, most English Puritans had not looked hard at questions of ecclesiastical polity since the days of Thomas Cartwright's early efforts in the 1570's and 1580's. Minor reforms, such as those requested of James I in 1604, were all that most Puritans dared hope for until the events of the 1640's. Then the chief Puritan spokesmen were largely Scots, who sought for England the kind of ecclesiastical government which they knew in Scotland. Among these was Robert Baillie, who took out on John Cotton some of the frustrations which he was experiencing at the Westminster Assembly. He attacked Cotton in *A Dissuasive from the Errours of the Time* (1645). Baillie identified Cotton and his ecclesiastical position with that of Separatism and Brownism; and he then identified Brownism with Anabaptism, which most Protestants regarded as the worst kind of radicalism and anarchism. Cotton's reply, *The Way of the Congregational Churches Cleared,* not published until 1648, is one of his most interesting works because much of it is autobiographical. Perhaps because he is defending himself and his cause at a time he knew to be crucial, Cotton wrote *The Way Cleared,* his most vigorous book. He intended it for the press, but doubtless he was unhappy that the author of the prefatory epistle saw the treatise not as a defense of the church polity which ought to be adopted, but as a means of demonstrating to the Presbyterians that the Congregationalists deserved to be accepted in church fellowship. Cotton's delay in answering his Presbyterian opponents with this work may well have been caused by his taking time the previous year to answer the attacks of Roger Williams. Now he had to reply to criticisms of his treatment of the Anne Hutchinson affair.

Cotton begins *The Way Cleared* with a description of the origins of modern Congregationalism, the term that appears to be Cotton's invention and that he prefers to the common English term, "Independency," since the latter is used by other groups such as the Baptists, the Seekers, and the Familists. For him the most important Separatist is not Robert Browne, founder of the Brownists, nor Henry Barrow, founder of the Barrowists, but John Robinson, pastor of the Plymouth Pilgrims when they were staying in Holland. Robinson was a Separatist, and, though he became only a moderate one, Cotton cannot approve of him. But he notes that the further reformation of the Church of England which Parliament and the Westminster Assembly had been making eliminated from the Church those features which had led to Robinson's separation.

Following the preliminary defense against the charge of

Separatism from the attacks of Baillie, Cotton next considers in a very important passage the history of his own group. This passage is worth quoting at length:

> That the separatists were our fathers, we have justly denied . . . seeing that they neither begat us to God, nor to the church, nor to their schism. That we are (through grace) begotten to God and to His church, we received (many of us) from the blessing of Christ upon the ministry of England. That we grew weary of the burden of episcopacy and conformity, we received from the Word of God by the help of the non-conformists there. That we laid aside the Book of Common Prayer, we received from the serious meditation of the Second Commandment, and not from the writings of the separatists, though they also had taken up the same conclusion upon other premises. The particular visible church of a congregation to be the first subject of the power of the keys, we received by the light of the Word from Mr. Parker, Mr. Baynes, and Dr. Ames, from whom also (from two of them at least) we received light out of the Word for the matter of the visible church to be visible saints, and for the form of it to be a mutual covenant, whether an explicit or implicit profession of faith and subjection to the Gospel of Christ in the society of the church or presbytery thereof. . . . And having received these, not from the separatists but from the Lord Jesus, by gracious saints and faithful witnesses of Jesus, the consanguinity of our tenents with any the like found amongst the separatists will not demonstrate the separatists to be our fathers (13).

Cotton thus identifies his tradition as being non-Separatist. He does admit, however, that the Bay Colony practice was influenced by the American Separatist camp at Plymouth: ". . . some of the first comers might help their theory by hearing and discerning their practice at Plymouth" (17). But Cotton tells his opponent that he himself had made a covenant with members of his congregation in Lincolnshire.

The sense of unity which these Congregationalists felt was, as Cotton indicates, a result of their common experiences. Paul Baynes and Robert Parker, both of whom died in 1617, were prominent, influential Puritans. Preacher at Great St. Andrew's Church in Cambridge from 1602, Baynes must have been well known to Cotton, to Thomas Hooker, and perhaps to John Winthrop, who studied at Cambridge and became a Puritan during Baynes's years there. William Ames (died 1633) arranged for the publication of Baynes's important posthumous *The Diocesans Trial* (1621), and he also translated into Latin in 1610 the even more important *English Puritanisme* of William Bradshaw. Thomas Hooker in turn edited Ames's last work, *A Fresh Suit against Human Ceremonies* (1633). Nearly all of the New England ministers came to America because they were Congregationalists; what Cotton calls "our tenents" had attracted, in old England, Hugh Peter, John Eliot, John Davenport, and all of the better-known ministers who were Cotton's contemporaries. This story is well told in Perry Miller's *Orthodoxy in Massachusetts*.

William Ames's most important work is *Medulla Sacrae Theologiae*; first published in 1623 and then translated into English, it was published at London in an undated edition, perhaps in 1638, as *The Marrow of Sacred Divinity*. A reading of this work is convincing proof that Cotton relied very heavily indeed on the light which Ames shed on the Word. In the *Marrow* is to be found almost everything that Cotton taught in his Congregational works, and the language is at times so close as to indicate that Cotton had Ames's book before him when he wrote. Ames insists, for example, that the church which Christ instituted is not "national, provincial, or diocesan . . . but it is parochial, or of one congregation . . ." (178). It is Ames who insists upon the importance of a church covenant, "whereby believers do particularly bind themselves together to perform all those duties . . . which pertain to the respect and edification of the church" (141). Ames teaches that a minister's ordination depends on his being called by a congregation (180), that excommunication requires the approval of the congregation (169-70), and that ministers are "either pastors and teachers, or ruling elders" (180). Cotton's teachings on synods, sacraments, and discipline reflect precisely what Ames's book proposes. Perhaps Cotton felt that, since Ames had intended to come to America but was stopped by death, it was up to him to say what Ames would have said.

Cotton continues his justification of himself and his career by crediting the coming of the Massachusetts Bay Company for the survival of the Massachusetts Indians, who had been severely weakened by a plague on the arrival of the whites. The Indians had not only survived, Cotton declares; they had the opportunity to hear the Christian gospel preached by John Eliot.

But the hope of extensive missionary successes that Cotton had expressed when he preached to the departing colonists of 1630 had vanished: until the ruin of Antichrist and the conversion of the Jews, only "some sprinklings and gleanings" of Indians could be converted (78).

A principal charge that Cotton was called to answer is that the Congregational system excludes "many thousand Christians whom they dare not deny to be truly religious of all the privileges of the church" (69). Cotton replies that everyone is allowed to attend all services; the Lord's Supper only is limited to church members. "Is it a dishonor to God," questions Cotton, "that such are withheld from the Lord's Table by whom the name of God is dishonored either through their ignorance or scandal?" (73). The godly are all admitted to some church; only the scandalous and those newly arrived and not yet known are not church members.

Here Cotton was being less than generous to the many who then lived in the Massachusetts Bay Colony but were not church members; these were always a majority, though from the earliest years of the Colony the least desirable immigrants had been shipped out of the Colony. Cotton was on stronger grounds when he answered the charge that no New England minister preached conversion sermons by citing the published works of Thomas Shepard and Thomas Hooker. (He did well not to spell out what they had preached: Shepard's popular *The Sincere Convert* is subtitled *Discovering the small number of True Believers, And the great difficulty of Saving Conversion.* Hooker was criticized in print for demanding too much of a man in the conversion process.)

What was separating the English Presbyterians and the American Congregationalists appears to have been the question of discipline. The Presbyterians and nearly all of the great Continental Reformed theologians supposed every citizen to be a member of the national church, a system that permitted the church to serve as custodian of the morals of the community. In New England the state served this function, and the church could be selective. But the New England policy was seen by the Presbyterians as a radical departure from the tradition, and Cotton strongly identified himself with the tradition. Consequently, we can understand why Cotton's defenses seem addressed almost as much to himself as to his opponents.

Cotton describes the relationship of the Congregational practices to the Reformed tradition thus:

> Though in the bishops' time we did not forthwith receive all the members of the Church of England into the fellowship of our churches, yet (for ought I know) we are not likely to stand aloof from Presbyterial churches faithfully administered, nor from the testimony which they shall give of their members, that may have occasion to traffic hither, and the like do I conceive of other Reformed churches in other nations of Christendom. Presbyterian churches faithfully administered are not wont to admit a mixed profane multitude to the Lord's Supper (90).

Cotton's technique in this defense seems to be to argue that the relationship of the churches would be no problem were all churches to be as faithfully administered as the New England churches.

But Cotton's chief precedent for the practices of New England Congregationalism is the way of the early church. The churches of the apostles, argues Cotton, were Congregational; and, during the first three Christian centuries, the examination of catechumens was so strict that no crimes could be charged against the Christians except their faith. The first departures from the way of the apostles occurred during the third century.

The Way Cleared is almost a formless book, for its arrangement is dictated largely by the order of the arguments which Cotton is answering. It contains, nevertheless, much of Cotton's very best prose, on the whole considerably better than what is found in the sermons. The gentleness which frequently makes the sermons rather tame is gone; instead, we find a remarkable vigor. One of the better passages is the following:

> For the fruits of Congregational discipline in England, they that walk in that way amongst you might speak far more particularly and largely than I here can do at such a remote distance. But if books and letters and reports do not too much abuse us with false intelligence, the great . . . victories whereby the Lord hath wrought salvation for England in these late wars have been as so many testimonies of the blessing of God upon our way. For the chief instruments which God hath delighted to use herein have been the faith and fidelity, the courage and constancy of Independents. And when I say Independents, I mean not those corrupt sects and heresies which shroud them-

selves under the vast title of Independency, and in the meantime cast off all church government and churches too, but such
as profess the Kingdom of Christ in the government of each holy
congregation of saints within themselves. Far be it from me to
undervalue the brotherly assistance of the Scottish churches
and commonwealth in working so great a deliverance for England. Yea, I account their concurrence a greater matter than
assistance in this great work. Their exemplary piety and zeal,
their courage and confidence in rising up and standing out
against the invasion of episcopal tyranny and superstition did
doubtless quicken and encourage England to stand for the like
liberty in the like cause and to put forth that zeal which the
Lord had kindled in the hearts of many for reformation. And
this was more than an assistance, even a guidance (103).

Controversial prose usually has a short life, but if Cotton is to
be remembered for his prose, he should be remembered for
passages like this one: emphatic, clear, and rhythmical.

The brief and much less interesting second part of *The Way
Cleared* is an answer to Samuel Rutherford, a Scottish divinity
professor who had seen *The Way of the Churches* in manuscript
and had published in reply *The Due Right of Presbyteries*
(1644), and to Daniel Cawdry, who had been more pugnacious
in his anonymous *Vindiciae Clavium* (1645). Against these two,
Cotton cites Scripture and argues logically to maintain that a
church exists by virtue of a covenant—not because it has proper
ministers. Cotton lines up his favorite authorities in his support:
Augustine, William Whitaker (1548-95), Paul Baynes, Junius
(1545-1602), and William Ames.

IX *Preface to* The Answer

In the same year that Cotton's *Way of the Congregational
Churches Cleared* was published, 1648, there appeared two other
important defenses of Congregationalism: Thomas Hooker's
Survey of the Summe of Church-Discipline and John Norton's
*Responsio ad totam questionum syllogen à Guilelmo Apollonio
propositam.* The former, the longest of the defenses of Congregationalism, was written several years earlier; but, lost in transit
to England, it had to be reconstructed by Hooker, then near
death. Norton's book was addressed to a Continental audience;

it was translated by Douglas Horton and published in 1958 as *The Answer to the Whole Set of Questions of the Celebrated Mr. William Apollonius.* Prefixed to this work is a letter from old England by the Independents Goodwin, Nye, and Simpson, and a letter from New England by John Cotton.

Cotton's letter is a most revealing document: it explains indirectly the reasons for Cotton's later painful sense of separation from his English colleagues. For non-conformists like himself, Cotton declared, only two choices existed in the England of the early 1630's: to perish in prison or to leave the country. The great Puritan leaders advised the latter, for "by the free preaching of the Word and the actual practice of our church discipline" the colonists could offer a great witness. If this was Cotton's mission, surely the course of English history was a disappointment to him; for not only did the English not follow his Congregational practices developed in America, but the advocates of Congregationalism in England adopted a policy of toleration, which Cotton abhorred.

X *The Cambridge Platform*

Because by definition Congregationalism had no central government, the *apologiae* which Cotton prepared were in no way official. They did not bind the churches of the New England Way, and they had not been adopted as official statements of either policy or procedure. Cotton was the self-appointed defender of Congregationalism. In the mid-1640's, however, circumstances demanded something more official; the consequence was the Cambridge Platform of 1648.

As early as 1643 a clergy conference held in Cambridge had disapproved of some of the Presbyterian features which were developing at Newbury, where the ministers wanted to take away from the church members the right of consultation and assent. Nevertheless, Presbyterianism continued to attract New Englanders, and it was of course dominating the Westminster Assembly. Perhaps from a desire to assert militantly their position, now in serious danger for the first time, some ministers in the spring of 1646 requested the General Court to call a synod. The General Court consequently invited the churches to confer for the "establishing and settling" of the right form of church government and discipline. The invitation reads, in part, as follows:

> Inasmuch as times of public peace, which by the mercy of God are vouchsafed to these plantations (but how long the same may continue we do not know) are much more commodious for the effecting of such a work than those troublesome times of war and public disturbances thereby, as the example of our dear native country doth witness at this day . . . and considering withal that, through want of the thing here spoken of, some differences of opinion and practice of one church from another do already appear amongst us . . . it is therefore thought expedient . . . that there be a public assembly of the elders and other messengers of the several churches within this jurisdiction. . . .[12]

The questions of baptism and church-membership were singled out as matters especially in need of discussion, for a group of New Englanders were petitioning Parliament for redress against the practices of the New England churches in these matters.

Sessions of the synod began in September, 1646, with discussions and, more important, with the appointment of a committee to prepare "a model of church government." Appointed were three ministers, Ralph Partridge, Richard Mather, and John Cotton. The synod then adjourned till 1647. As the meetings proceeded, the power shifted from Presbyterians to Independents in England; and the pressure was removed from the synod to declare itself plainly on the vexing questions of church membership and baptism.

Finally in 1648 the synod adopted a statement by Richard Mather, who drew heavily on Cotton's writings as well as on his own; the result was the Cambridge Platform, or, as the work was entitled when published the next year, *A Platform of Church Discipline Gathered out of the Word of God and Agreed upon by the Elders and Messengers of the Churches Assembled in the Synod at Cambridge in New England.* It was prefaced by an important statement by John Cotton. In time the *Platform* was accepted by most of the churches and by the General Court. It is thus an official statement of the New England Way. Though soon in need of extensive revision, it has been called by Walker in *Creeds of Congregationalism* (185) "the most important monument of early New England Congregationalism." It was reprinted again and again, thirty-four times in all, the latest as recently as 1943.

As has been said, the *Platform* reflects much of Cotton's teachings on Congregationalism. The extent of Mather's borrowing may be suggested by these parallel passages concerning the relationship of one church to another:

Platform	*The Keyes Of the Kingdom*
By way of consultation one with another when we have occasion to require judgment and counsel of other churches, touching any person or cause wherewith they may be better acquainted than ourselves. As the church of Antioch consulted with the apostles and elders of the church at Jerusalem, about the question of circumcision of the Gentiles . . . (Walker, *Creeds of Congregationalism*, 230).	By way of consultation, one church hath liberty of communicating with another to require their judgment and counsel touching any persons or cause wherewith they may be better acquainted than themselves. Thus the church of Antioch by their messengers consulted with the church at Jerusalem, touching the necessity of circumcision (18).

Cotton's preface shows him in his role as diplomat. He professes that the New England churches are eager for fellowship with the Presbyterians and have consequently accepted "for substance of doctrine" the Westminster Confession prepared at the Assembly in England. Thereby the New England churches have proved themselves innocent of heresy, and Cotton hopes that the Presbyterians will not think them guilty of schism for "a different apprehension of the mind of Christ . . . in some few points touching church order" (Walker, 195-96). He begins with great modesty and humility.

Cotton then speaks hopefully of how "the example of such poor outcasts as ourselves" (196) may help prevent extensive internal squabbles among the English Puritans. He supposes that English churchmen might be reluctant for American practices to be used in England because of three disadvantages which apparently had been brought to his attention. First, Congregationalism would despoil the parish churches by attracting all of their best members. Second, Congregationalism would provide no means of disciplining non-members who are ignorant and scandalous. Third, it would create divisions among families, for members would belong to several churches.

These problems Cotton had not dealt with before, for earlier he had advocated the establishment of Congregational churches as the sole churches of England; now he considers them as co-existing with Presbyterian churches. Cotton's answers to these three criticisms seem at first to reveal a far more tolerant spirit than he had shown before in his works. He argues, for example, that it is wrong for members to desert Presbyterian churches because of their government. But he goes on to say that they should remain only "To convince their brethren of their sinful defects and duly wait for their reformation" (198). What he advocates seems to the modern reader a scheme for introducing fifth-columnists into the English Presbyterian churches.

Another arrangement which Cotton suggests for getting around the criticism is membership in two churches. In this fashion Congregationalists can "either after or before the public assembly of the parish take an opportunity to gather together for the administration of the sacraments and censures and other church ordinances amongst themselves" (199). At any rate, Cotton suggests, if the Presbyterians should lose members to the Congregational churches, "it will never grieve the holy hearts of godly ministers that their hearers should follow after Christ" (199). Thus, though he appears to have a desire for fellowship with the Presbyterians, Cotton in fact cannot imagine a situation in which the Congregationalists do not have some sort of superiority.

The second objection—that of discipline of non-members—Cotton deals with in an even less satisfactory way, at least for anyone who knows what went on in the Massachusetts of Cotton's day. Cotton thinks that the churches provide discipline for non-members since they are required to attend services and since the ministers and the church members tell them of their failings. The non-members listen respectfully, for "they see no hope of enjoying church-fellowship or participation in the sacraments for themselves or their children" unless they win the approval of ministers and members (201).

The third objection—familial division—Cotton can answer with greater ease. Good family relations are encouraged by Congregationalism since one of the qualifications for church membership is the good testimony of one's family and the report that one's family is what it should be.

Cotton's closing effort to create good feelings between Presbyterians and Congregationalists is not likely to be regarded as successful by anyone who has read the casuistry of the early portions of the preface. In many ways the preface of the Cambridge Platform is one of the most disturbing of Cotton's writings. The idealism which seemed to permeate his earlier Congregational writings has vanished; he seems now only a diehard, old-school sectarian.

XI   Of the Holiness of Church Members

By 1650 toleration was permitted for all the English, but Cotton was still defending Congregationalism, partly because his commitment to the church polity which he had done so much to formulate was one of the factors that prevented his returning to England. In the prefatory letter to *Of the Holinesse of Church Members* (1650), addressed to the people of Boston in Lincolnshire, Cotton acknowledged the faithfulness of his former parishioners who had annually remembered Cotton's financial needs; but he urged them to recognize that, since his old church admits as members people other than "professed saints," he cannot return as their minister. He cites as well his age (sixty-six) and his American obligations, but he is most concerned with their open policy on church membership. The treatise which follows is Cotton's effort to help them eliminate their error. But it is, as Cotton acknowledges, another volley in the battle between himself and his Scottish Presbyterian opponents Robert Baillie and Samuel Rutherford. The treatise is so sophisticated that one suspects Cotton pretty much forgot his former parishioners in the course of composition.

Cotton was writing at a time when the New England churches had already begun lowering their standards for membership, but he was prepared to insist—and on this point he may well have been addressing his New England colleagues—that there is a point beyond which a church could not go and still remain a true church. It is not enough to demand what all of the Reformed churches demanded: the pure Word of God purely preached, sacraments duly administered, discipline maintained according to God's Word, and members externally professing their faith. In addition Cotton demanded that church members give evidence that they are effectually called, elected, and justified. In fact, however, Cotton merely interpreted one word more strictly than his fellows in this definition of a true visible church. The word is "duly." The sacraments are not duly administered, argued Cotton, unless they are administered to the right people. Nor can discipline be said to exist where the wrong people are admitted to the church. The only corrupt persons who can be members are those whose corruption has just been recognized and who therefore are about to be cut off. Cotton describes what he conceives to be a typical case:

> . . . suppose a man born and baptized in the church, after he be grown . . . do continue grossly and securely ignorant of the principles of religion, I suppose such an one may justly be esteemed unregenerate (for without knowledge the mind cannot be good), and being such he may justly be debarred from the fellowship of the Lord's Table and such other church privileges as be peculiar to confirmed members. Suppose further, that such a person being admonished by the elders and brethren of the church for his gross ignorance do nevertheless still continue in gross ignorance and in neglect of [the] means of instruction, and (as is the wont of such) suppose he be known to neglect family duties, prayer, catechising of his household, examination of their profiting by public ordinances, and shall after admonition for these known defects still continue in his ignorance and negligence, and that after public rebukes for the same before the church, I demand whether such a person may not justly be cast out of the church for his unregeneration and these offensive fruits of it? (57).

Cotton himself was very reluctant to use the discipline of excommunication; in the years from 1634 to 1652, only five members of his church were excommunicated. Excommunication was almost complete ostracism. When Mrs. William Hibbins was excommunicated, Pastor John Wilson pronounced:

> I do exclude you not only from the fellowship of the church in all the public ordinances of the same, but also from private fellowship and communion with any servants of God in the church, except only in those relations to your own family: to your husband, children, and servants. And for the greater terror

and amazing of you, I do here in the name of Christ Jesus and His church deliver you up to Satan and to his power and working; that you which would not be guided by the counsels of God may be terrified and hampered by the snares and powers of Satan for the destruction of your proud flesh, for the humbling of your soul, that your spirit may be saved in the day of the Lord Jesus if it be His blessed will. And so as an unclean beast I pronounce you an excommunicate person.[13]

Readmission after excommunication was not painfully difficult.

It was on admission rather than excommunication that Cotton focused his attention, and for admission he continued to demand public confession of sins, profession of faith, and declaration of willingness to be subject to Christ.

XII Certain Queries *and* A Defense

Cotton's last published thoughts on Congregationalism are contained in *Certain Queries Tending to Accommodation and Communion of Presbyterian & Congregational Churches,* a work which he completed just before his death in 1652. Published in 1655 as part of *The Covenant of Grace,* it has its own title page, dated 1654. In the work Cotton displays a somewhat more liberal attitude toward the relationship of the two kinds of churches, probably because of his continuing disillusionment with English Independents. Now Cotton was prepared to admit that Presbyterian congregations are true churches if they have proper preaching and the truth of the Gospel, and if they are "not overgrown with ignorant and scandalous persons" (1) and if the congregations call their ministers. He considers the Presbyterians to be closer to the truth now, but he denies that Presbyterian ministers can be considered true and their sacraments valid unless they become more discriminate as to who is admitted to the Lord's Supper and unless they restrict the power of the elders over churches other than the ones to which they minister. Cotton takes back with one hand what he appeared to give away with the other.

Unexpectedly, Cotton foresees intercommunion between Congregationalists and Presbyterians, for an "error in judgment about discipline is not an heresy against the foundation of Christian religion" (8). This attitude is indeed an about-face for Cotton, to whom church discipline had been quite as important as doctrine. (In *The Bloudy Tenent, Washed* [1647], he had argued that "the matter and form" of the church was a fundamental of religion in the same class with the doctrine of the resurrection of the body.)

Another late work is *A Defence of Mr. John Cotton From the Charge of Selfe Contradiction,* with a long preface by John Owen. This work, written in answer to Daniel Cawdrey's *Inconsistency of the Independent Way* (1651), shows that seeming inconsistencies between Cotton's *Way of the Churches,* his *Keyes Of the Kingdom,* and his *The Way Cleared,* and Thomas Hooker's *Survey of the Summe of Church-Discipline* are merely verbal differences. This work has, however, little interest or importance.

Cotton's Congregational works had an importance in his own time which it is difficult to appreciate today. The Puritans' efforts in the 1640's to complete the reformation of the Church of England were the culmination of the work of nearly a hundred years. Through the press, Cotton was the chief spokesman for the Congregational interpretation of the Bible on church government. With toleration the order of the day in England and with the discovery in New England that Cotton's Congregationalism was unworkable, these works soon lost their importance. Today their chief value is the light they shed on the first generation of settlers in Massachusetts Bay, its ideals and aspirations.

CHAPTER 5

The Means of Grace:
The American Sermons

HOWEVER SUBSTANTIAL Cotton's reputation was as a preacher in England, he loomed a larger star in America. Benjamin Woodbridge, a Harvard graduate who returned to England to become a preacher of note, called Cotton

> A man of might, at heavenly eloquence,
> To fix the ear and charm the conscience,
> As if Apollos were reviv'd in him,
> Or he had learned of a seraphim.
> (Cotton Mather, *Magnalia
> Christi Americana* [1702], III, 31)

Although Cotton shared the pulpit of his church in the Bay Colony with John Wilson, New England practices provided plenty of opportunity for him to preach. On the Sabbath Wilson preached in the morning and Cotton in the afternoon, except during Cotton's second year. Then he did all the preaching, for Wilson had returned to England on business. In addition Cotton preached every other Thursday and on many special occasions, such as at the time of elections.

I   The Covenant of Grace

Perhaps the earliest of Cotton's American sermons which are extant are those published under the titles *The New Covenant* (1654), *The Covenant of Grace* (1655), and *A Treatise of the Covenant* (1659). The first volume was published with Cotton's consent after he had read and corrected it. The third volume was likewise corrected by the author, yet the 1659 edition is a third longer than the first edition. The explanation is that both volumes were made from notes. The epistle to the 1659 edition, which I have used, refers to "the diversity of amanuenses, who did take the notes of his sermons, some writing the same more largely and exactly than others. . . ." It is difficult to imagine why these sermons, which appear from their subject matter to have been delivered about 1636 (just before the outbreak of the Anne Hutchinson controversy), were not published earlier. The editors, perhaps, thought of this publication as a memorial tribute.

Turning to this volume after reading the several collections of Cotton's English sermons, one notices several differences. First, the sermons seem to have been prepared for a congregation more theologically sophisticated than Cotton's English audiences; there is a precision and care about knotty points of theology not found earlier. Second, Cotton preaches a stricter, more "Calvinistic" theology than he had earlier. Because of the time when they were preached and the great care which they usually show, these are among Cotton's most important sermons.

Cotton's text for all of these sermons is Acts 7:8: "and He gave him the covenant of circumcision, and so Abraham begat Isaac, and circumcised him the eighth day, and Isaac begat Jacob, and Jacob begat the twelve patriarchs." In this passage Cotton finds the idea of the continuing covenant of God and man, a covenant based not on works, as was the covenant with Adam, but on faith. The central concepts of the covenant of faith, or of grace, have already been considered in Chapter 4. But here Cotton makes clearer the relationship of Jesus Christ to the covenant: "God gave Himself to be a God to Abraham and to his seed, and received Abraham and his seed to be a people unto Himself, and the chiefest of this seed, the Lord Jesus Christ, He took to be the mediator or surety of this covenant between them both" (3). The idea of covenant may seem to imply some kind of rational understanding between God and man by which God agrees not to be altogether arbitrary in His decisions as to who shall be saved and who shall be damned. Cotton teaches, however, that in the agreement God keeps not only His own part of the contract but man's also. The contract is not conditional but absolute, for God is absolute and has involved Himself with both sides of the agreement.

To bring man into the covenant, God takes four steps. First, He separates him from his sins and passions by showing him that they are delivering him to damnation. Second, He shows man that he can have no confidence in his own works. Third, He "taketh up His seat in the soul" (19). Finally by His Spirit He works faith in the soul so that it receives Jesus Christ: ". . . the Spirit of God taking possession in our hearts and working this faith in us, thereby we submit unto the Lord, and this is faith in Jesus Christ, that maketh us one with Christ, for our effectual calling bringeth us to be one with Him" (21).

As Cotton describes the process, it thus has distinct stages; and man is not within the covenant until he has been given faith, the fourth step. For this crucial gift God prepares a man through the previous steps. Later Cotton cautiously adds: "Reserving due honor to such gracious and precious saints as may be otherwise minded, I confess I do not discern that the Lord worketh and giveth any saving preparation in the heart till He give union with Christ [Cotton's fourth step], for if the Lord do any saving qualification before Christ, then the soul may be in the state of salvation before Christ, and that seemeth to be prejudicial unto the grace and truth of Jesus Christ" (39-40). The key phrase here is *saving qualification,* a phrase that suggests that entrance to the Covenant of Grace is conditional. For Cotton there can be no qualifying for grace.[1]

It has been supposed that the "precious saints" to whom Cotton refers include Thomas Hooker, who speaks of preparation as "a saving work, and a work of the Spirit" (*The Soules Preparation* [1632], 157). But both Hooker and Cotton teach that God prepares a man for faith and union with Christ, and both also teach that the process is wholly God's, not man's. Hooker does indeed teach that a man who is prepared for Christ and who dies is saved, but he also explains that "When the heart is fitted and prepared, the Lord Christ comes immediately into it" (*Soules Preparation,* 155).

In his English sermons Cotton maintained that sanctification is a good evidence of one's election. At that time he neglected the possibility that, by urging a man to look to his works as evidence that he was justified, he might induce him to seek his salvation by these works rather than by faith. Such a possibility seems to have been brought home to Cotton when he found that his own doctrine of the intimate connection of church and commonwealth was leading the magistrates, whose concern was of course civil discipline, to emphasize morality as *the* proof of piety: in Larzer Ziff's words "to believe that morality argued piety and that without morality there was no piety."[2] Cotton's doctrine that the state should be governed by those gifted with grace, the church members, did indeed emphasize sanctification.

At any rate, in *A Treatise of the Covenant of Grace* he urged his hearers to beware of judging the state of their souls by their power to perform good works. In the Covenant of Works, Cotton warns, God gives a temporary kind of sanctification, so that good works are "no evidence or witness of our union with Christ" (43). To tell the difference between this sanctification and the kind which follows justification is "a matter so narrow that the angels in Heaven have much ado to discern who differ" (44). "So glorious may this common sanctification be that it may dazzle the eyes of the best of God's children" (54).

The real test, Cotton now urges, is the nature of one's faith: ". . . the true sanctification of a sincere Christian is not discernable until he first discern his justifying faith" (55). This is precisely the position which Cotton took in his dispute with his clerical colleagues in the Anne Hutchinson case. Cotton does not neglect the fact that the doctrine of proof helps prevent any relaxation of effort: those who have a true faith, he teaches, feel the need for greater faith; those who have a temporary faith are confident of their faith.

In his belief that assurance of salvation comes through discerning one's faith, Cotton follows Calvin. In his explanation of the difficulty of distinguishing true sanctification from the sanctification which observance of the Law creates, Cotton follows Perkins. The position which he rejects is that of Calvin's successor, Theodore Beza.[3]

Next Cotton raises a vital question. If the salvation process does not require man's cooperation—the Arminian position which Cotton rejects—of what use are the promises? (An example of what Cotton calls the promises is John 3:16, "For God so loved the world that He gave His only begotten Son, that whosoever believeth in Him should not perish but have everlasting life.") These promises instruct, Cotton answers; they show the source of life and salvation. But also—and here Cotton appears to have trapped himself—they are useful for exhortation, "to stir up the sons of men . . . to provoke themselves and one another to look after the Lord" (65). But, Cotton confesses, the promises, which are able to appeal outwardly only, can do nothing without the working of the Spirit inwardly. As we have seen, Puritan preachers such as Cotton demanded that their hearers exert themselves, for the preachers hoped that God would use their words as the means of grace. Here presumably Cotton hoped that his teaching concerning the promises would be matched with the coming of the Spirit, for Cotton declares that the actual union of Christ and the soul comes through the promises. Cotton's mistake was in demanding action at the same time that he denied man's ability to act.

Cotton's new awareness of the validity of High Calvinist doctrines shines through the whole volume. It is perhaps best illustrated by his passage concerning church members' children who are not effectually called by God. The Lord, preaches Cotton.

> doth not only call them to church liberty and fellowship nor only bestow upon them sundry gifts of grace and great bounties and manifold preservation from evil, but likewise He doth offer them the sure mercies of David, for so God doth distinguish the sure mercies of the covenant. Isaiah lv.3, "Incline your ear and come unto me; hearken and your soul shall live, and I will make an everlasting covenant with you, even the sure mercies of David." Wherein you see the Lord putteth it upon such terms that if the soul come not by it, it is because he would not—not that any can come when they will, as by the power of their own will, but this the Lord will leave upon the children of Christian parents, that they shall not say that God forsook them until they have forsaken Him, and that when there lay no necessity upon them but voluntarily they did despise the grace of the covenant, for do but observe the causes wherefore the Lord hath discovenanted the children of gracious parents (222).

The grace given to those who are within the Covenant of Grace through their parents, "federal" grace, is not saving grace, and not such that "any can come [to God] when they will, as by the power of their own will," yet those who do not come have "forsaken Him," for "voluntarily they did despise the grace of the covenant"! Passages such as this are rare among Cotton's other writings; here his new strict Calvinism got the best of him and he delivered nonsense such as one cannot find in the writings of Calvin or of Augustine. Cotton seems to suppose that he can offer contradictory statements without admitting that he has given us a paradox. We can only observe that, though he rejected salvation by works as unchristian, preaching pure grace seemed too dangerous for him; it left too little for man to do.

Cotton has much to say in these sermons about the inadequacy of good works as evidence of salvation, but some other of his teachings must have been intended to warn the Antinomians of the limits of orthodoxy. He argues at length that his hearers should not look for "any revelation out of [aside from] the Word, for the Spirit comes in the mouth of the Word, and the Word in the mouth of the Spirit" (201). Yet the Spirit works "by a power above the Word" (215). Thus there can be no immediate divine revelation.

This volume of sermons suggests the validity of the thesis presented by Frank Hugh Foster that the reason for the failure of New England Puritanism was the preachers' emphasis on man's inability to act. The old saw that Puritans spoke like Arminians in the pulpit and like strict predestinarians in prayer does not hold true of these sermons. It is understandable that Foster should find the more Calvinistic of the Puritan preachers "all very gloomy" but think Cotton's earlier *The Way of Life* "rather helpful."[4]

II A Brief Exposition of Canticles (*1655*)

We noted that in England Cotton preached on the Song of Solomon and that his sermons were published in 1642. At an undetermined time during his American years Cotton turned again to that Old Testament book, which must have been a favorite since he chose a passage from it for his first American sermon in 1633. The American sermons, not published until 1655, were entitled *A Brief Exposition With Practical Observations Upon the Whole Book of Canticles. Never before Printed.* This time Cotton sees three levels of meaning. The work describes the relationship of Christ and the church in general, that of Christ and every sincere Christian soul, and the state of the church from Solomon's time to the Last Judgment. As he had devoted his efforts to the third of these in the earlier sermons, he now spends most of his time on the first two.

Cotton translates the erotic poetry of the book into the story of a love affair between himself and his congregation. "Let him kiss me with the kisses of his mouth" is the text which Cotton takes most delight in. First he explains that "kiss of his mouth" means "not of His lip . . . not dumb salutations, but vocal and lively significations and declarations of His love in His Word." Then he explains that the kisses are delivered not only through the prophets but through those who "interpret and apply them [the Scriptures] faithfully . . ." (2). In other words, sermons deliver kisses. And men return God's kisses "when we receive His Word with faith, love, joy, obedience" (3). Since Christ kisses through sermons, those who love Him most long for more sermons, and those whom Christ finds most beautiful are they "that seek Him in the purity of His public ordinances" (4).

These sermons are indeed a strange mixture. There is evangelism here, analysis of the conversion process, history, theology, folklore, all combined with exegesis. Verse 7:2—"Thy navel is like a round goblet, which wanteth not liquor; thy belly is like an heap of wheat, set about with lilies"—gets a typical treatment: the passage is interpreted as a discussion of baptism and the Lord's Supper!

Some of Cotton's interpretations of the Song of Solomon as church history also seem farfetched. He interprets 2:2—"as the lily among thorns, so is my love among the daughters"—as a refutation of "the popish exception against the visibility of our church before Luther" (37). He comments on "King Solomon made himself a chariot of the wood of Lebanon" (3:9) that, since the passage means that Christ made Himself mediator, here the Scripture tells us "the Virgin Mary, nor any saint or angel did never make themselves such a chariot; Christ made this chariot for Himself. He admits no companion to ride with Him in it" (76).

Cotton explains v.15, "His legs are as pillars of marble": "These two legs (historically) were John Huss and Hierom of Prague . . ." (156). The next step in the Reformation is described in 6:6: "My beloved is gone down into his garden"; down because it is in a lower condition than some of Christ's other gardens. "Wittenberg was a meaner place than Rome or Constantinople

or Alexandria or Jerusalem or Antioch, where Christ had formerly His pleasant gardens" (164).

With this kind of inspired approach, Cotton manages to find
occasion to discuss how Christ prepares the soul for His coming,
the duties of church members, the conversion of the Jews, the
state of the English churches, and contemporary Congregationalism. He supposes that since 8:13 says, "Thou dwellest in
gardens," Christ intended each church to be a separate entity.
He finds occasion to chide the New England churches: "Time
was when it was thus with New English churches; but now we
cannot bear wrongs, but grow contentious in suits. Now few
come to us. Those that come, they corrupt us" (213).

The most unconvincing discussion is Cotton's argument that
8:11-12 reveals Christ's relationship to His church "by a com-
parison of unequals or things unlike" (229). Since Solomon had
a remote vineyard, Christ keeps His church under close watch.
Since Solomon handed over responsibility for his vineyard to
keepers, Christ keeps the church in His own hand. Solomon's
keepers paid him in money; Christ keeps all the increase of His
vineyard to Himself.

All in all Cotton's commentary is the most peculiar of his
works. One pictures the Boston minister in his study, happy to
be away from the world of controversy, ferreting out meanings
from this great love poem with the greatest sense of mission and
accomplishment. He was, after all, following in an old tradition
of exegesis, as his successor at St. Botolph's in Lincolnshire,
Anthony Tuckney, points out in his prefatory epistle. But one may
choose, as did Tuckney, to be a bit skeptical of the value of
Cotton's scholarship.

III Brief Exposition of Ecclesiastes

Among his posthumous works is Cotton's *Briefe Exposition with
Practical Observations upon the Whole Book of Ecclesiastes,* also
arranged for publication by Tuckney. The work is of interest
because of what it reveals not only about Cotton but also about
the state of mind of early New England. As early as the 1640's
there was to be found in New England congregations a disturbing new complacency that led Cotton to address to his people
the lessons taught by the preacher to whom all was vanity.

Cotton addresses his audience as those who left old England and their worldly goods for the sake of their religion but who now are ready to leave their religion in New England for the sake of their worldly goods. But if this leads us to expect drama and specific details about the worldliness of Cotton's parishioners, we are soon disappointed. For Cotton begins his analysis by revealing that he belongs to the tradition of the pharisaical commentators on the Scripture, not to the tradition of the prophets. In the opening lines, "Vanity of vanities, saith the preacher, vanity of vanities, all is vanity," Cotton discovers eleven ornaments of rhetoric: hyperbole, polyptoton, epizeuxis, anadiplosis, epanalepsis, anaphora, epistrophe, epanodos, numerous oratorius, climax, and paranomasia.

This kind of commentary does not strike the reader as morally edifying. Perhaps Cotton's hearers found more guidance in the interesting idea that in being idle one can manage to break five of the Ten Commandments without lifting a finger. One thus breaks the commandment against using God's name in vain, in that idleness means spending one's time and talents in vain; the commandment against working on the Sabbath, since one cannot honor the Sabbath by resting unless one has first been laboring; the commandment to honor one's parents, since Proverbs 10:5 warns that a prudent son gathers in summer (presumably being a prudent son is one way of honoring one's parents); the commandment against killing, since idleness is self-murder; the commandment against adultery because Sodom is described in Ezekiel 16:49 as being guilty of "prosperous ease" (a case of guilt by association); the commandment against stealing because Proverbs 19:15 says that an idle person will suffer hunger and Proverbs 10:4 says that a slack hand causes poverty.

At times Cotton manages to interpret the text in a straightforward way. In his text he sees the warning that man should view the study of the world as a proper duty but only as a means to becoming a better person. But one is much more struck by the strange and esoteric interpretations, such as the one of Ecclesiastes 12:12: "And further, by these, my son, be admonished: of many books there is no end, and much study is a weariness of the flesh." For Cotton this passage refutes the concept that we should add to the Scriptures the decrees of the Popes, the Apocrypha, the Canons of the Councils, and the traditions of the Church Fathers as further directions for faith and living.

Cotton's concerns are not only rhetoric, ethics, and pro-Protestant scriptural interpretation but also science. He finds a confutation of Copernicus in the familiar "The sun also riseth, and the sun goeth down," and he adds: "If the earth moved swiftly, when a man throweth a stone the same way the earth moveth, he might easily overtake the stone before it fell." For him the sun and the stars are alive: they must be since they move themselves. And Aristotle was wrong to think that water seeks a lower level.

The natural order of the universe is a providential order; a man can understand God's dealings with him by observing what he is doing when some evil occurs to him, a view which seems inconsistent with Cotton's view of the heathen moral philosophers, who are for him "vain and wicked."

Ecclesiastes seems to have been for Cotton the occasion to discuss anything that interested him. We find, for example, his favorite idea that magistrates are required to put to death all blasphemers, Jewish and Christian apostates to idolatry, witches, and seducers to idolatry; for, though no man has a coercive power over another's conscience, men should be punished for sinning against their own consciences.

Cotton finds Scripture an invaluable source of answers to questions, but one may be permitted the suspicion that the answers he found were ones which he was predisposed to find. He learns that Solomon is in Heaven by noting that in Luke 13:28 Jesus says that all prophets are in Heaven, and from II Peter 1:19-21 and Ephesians 2:20 that the whole of Scripture was written by prophets and apostles. (The passage of Peter reads, "We have also a more sure word of prophecy; whereunto ye do well that ye take heed, as unto a light that shineth in a dark place, until the day dawn, and the daystar arise in your hearts: Knowing this first, that no prophecy of the Scripture is of any private interpretation. For the prophecy came not in old time by the will of man: but holy men of God spake as they were moved by the Holy Ghost." Ephesians reads, "And [ye] are built upon the foundation of the apostles and prophets, Jesus Christ Himself being the chief cornerstone.")

Cotton interprets the memorable first nine verses of Ecclesiastes 3, beginning "To everything there is a season, and a time to every purpose under the heavens," to mean that for everything there is a limited time. On the phrase "a time to dance" Cotton is explicit: "It is not said there is a lawful time but a limited time."

Ecclesiastes contains some notable statements of skepticism, but Cotton's commentary nearly overlooks them. One example may suffice. In Ecclesiastes 3:21 we read: "Who knoweth the spirit of man that goeth upward, and the spirit of the beast that goeth downward to the earth?" Cotton recognizes that the passage says that the difference between what happens to a dead man and to a dead animal "is not known or acknowledged, discerned, or considered by men generally, to wit, not by natural man at all." Yet he also uses the passage as a refutation of the concept that the spirits of the Patriarchs descended to limbo: "here we see the souls of men before Christ's resurrection went upward."

The *Exposition . . . upon . . . Ecclesiastes* is not one of Cotton's more important books. Although it does reveal Cotton the scholar who is remote from the problems of ordinary men, it is not memorable for its prose or for its thoughts. Moreover, it does not even have much of that quality which makes some of Cotton's writing interesting, a peculiar habit of thought which is fascinating in its fantasticality.

IV   An Exposition of Revelation 13

The height of Cotton's fantasy comes in the commentaries on the thirteenth and sixteenth chapters and on two verses of the twentieth chapter of Revelation. But we have a better reason to be interested in these works, for in them Cotton reveals most clearly his understanding of his own times and of his own mission in history. The prefatory epistle describes *An Exposition upon The Thirteenth Chapter of the Revelation* as weekly lectures delivered at the end of 1639 and the beginning of 1640; the work was not published until 1655.

Cotton recognizes that Revelation is an obscure book but testifies that "so much light God casts almost into the head of every man that takes this book in hand . . . that He adds some light more than hath been before brought to his hand" (4). The light that Cotton finds enables him to explain that the seven-headed beast described in 13:1 is the Roman Catholic Church, its seven heads being the seven hills and the seven kingly governments of Rome; the sea from which it arose is the corrupt doctrine, tumult and contention from which the Roman Catholic Church arose. After more of this kind of characterization, much of it quite ingenious, Cotton concludes: "The visible Catholic Roman Church is in the esteem of the Holy Ghost a monstrous beast" (14).

Cotton then contrasts this beast with the church which he says the Lord instituted, as described in Matthew 18:15-18, the church to which one is to tell of his brother's offenses as a last resort. "What!" exclaims Cotton, "The catholic visible church! When will that meet, think you? And is it ever to be expected that when they do meet, that every brother of this country and other countries must go to Rome and tell the trespasses of his brother against him, and send for those that have offended him, and thus and thus plead with them?" (15).

From this monstrous church, Cotton declares, God has delivered his followers, but also from "the remnants of the image of this beast, from all diocesan and national churches, and from metropolitan and catholic visible churches that are images of this great beast" (18). But those remaining behind in England still may suffer excommunication for going to hear a sermon away from home when at home they can hear no sermons.

Though he finds much to observe in all of these verses of Revelation (13:3 he sees as the history of the Catholic Church at the beginning of the Dark Ages), Cotton excuses his failure to make additional comments on these lines, for, says he, "I affect brevity in mystical Scripture" (47). Instead, he focuses on contemporary Catholicism.

Four reasons for the admiration which people give to the Roman Church are these, according to Cotton. First, men have wrongly interpreted parts of Scripture, such as Peter's being given the keys. Second, Catholicism corresponds to what man's corrupt reason wants. Third, priests, monks, and friars, by preaching hell-fire and damnation, arouse the people's fears; then they offer relief by masses, pardons, and pilgrimages. Fourth, the councils and synods gave reverence to Rome.

After various excoriations of Roman Catholicism, Cotton comes to Revelation 13:5, the latter part of which he finds as "obscure as any place in the Word" (80). The passage reads: ". . . and power was given unto him [the beast] to continue forty and two months." Cotton justifies his labor in explaining the passage: "I would not busy myself in needless speculations, but I find not any word of God a needless speculation for the church to search into and understand" (83). Cotton argues that the author of Revelation refers to 1260 days when he writes of forty-two months; he did not use the term *days* because it was not appropriate when referring to the work of darkness, and Cotton concludes that days here equal years, for the Old Testament prophets often refer to days when they mean years. The question is, 1260 years beginning when? Cotton believes that the period began in 395, when the Pope was first called Pontifex Maximus, but it also began at the time of Constantine. He therefore concludes that the ending is the year of the Pope's Bull against Elizabeth (1570), *and also* 1655, when Cotton foresees a great blow to Catholicism.

At times Cotton's attitude toward Catholicism is surprisingly like some twentieth-century attitudes toward Communism. After offering his interpretation of the forty-two months, Cotton suggests that this text

> may teach all the saints in this country or wherever not to trust the pretenses of deceitful men, especially such as are not sound in religion, and take heed also how you trust upon your own strength. (Let me put them both together for brevity's sake.) We know not how soon any of us may be tempted in this kind, what wars may be raised against this country (though we have none for the present, nor fear none), yet in time we know not what may come. What, are we better than our fathers? The Beast of Rome still lives; his forty-two months is not yet out (though his power be much weakened), but his agents still live (110).

Cotton attacks Roman Catholicism because it is "composed to natural sense": it appeals to the eye with its images, pictures, temples, and vestments; to the ear with its vocal and instrumental music; to the nose with its incense and perfumes; to the taste with its feasts; and to the touch by its toleration of houses of prostitution and its light penance for lewdness. He attacks Roman Catholicism also because it is attractive to natural reason. It teaches a historical faith (such as devils may have); an implicit faith (so that a man has only to believe whatever his church believes); repentance based only on contrition, confession, and satisfaction; the concept that man can keep the Law and work out his own salvation but that his salvation must remain uncertain; and a form of church government that results in unity and order.

Because Roman Catholicism has such an appeal, the Catholic Church, Cotton acknowledges, is very large; and Congregationalism as a form of church government is very rare. For Congregationalism is based on the ordinances of Christ, not those of men—and corrupt men prefer their own devices.

The reference to the Book of Life (Revelation 13:8) raises the question, Are only church members' names written in the Book? According to Cotton, the register of members of Congregational churches and the Book of Life will be found "not exactly agreeing," for "sometimes we put in more than God doth, and sometimes less. There be [those] that belong to life whom we do not receive. Others . . . do not present themselves or we do not receive [them] through some failings in them or us, but if they belong to life, they are written in the Lamb's Book of Life" (133). On the other hand, no Roman Catholic's name will be found in the Book; "if they die in that religion" they "cannot go beyond a reprobate" (144), a teaching in which Cotton follows William Perkins.

The discussion of the Book of Life inspired one of Cotton's most picturesque passages:

> When the Lord wrote down thy name, or mine, or any man's name, who stood by at His elbow (if I may so speak) to put Him in mind of my name or thine? He thought of us, if our names be there, and He set us down, and He delivered us to Christ Jesus by name. Whatever thy name is, He took notice of thy name. Such a man in such a place, he will live in this or that country. He is one; take notice of him; lay down a price for him. In fulness of time send a spirit into his heart. If he live in a popish country, save him from popery. If in a worldly country, save him from the world. Wherever he lives, save him from himself and bring him to my heavenly kingdom (146).

Had Cotton written often in this vein, his sermons would justify his contemporary reputation.

Cotton finds the phrase "the Lamb slain from the foundation of the world" (Revelation 13:8) particularly rich in meaning. If Christ was slain from the foundation of the world in terms of the efficacy and virtue of His death, then it was efficacious for such Old Testament figures as Abel, Joseph, Enoch, and Abraham. Since Enoch is said to have walked with God, he must have been one of those who benefited from Christ's death. Faith must thus have existed from Eve's time, and its object was Christ. If Christ was slain from the foundation of the world, then the world was depraved from the beginning; depravity is the universal human condition. "Folly is bound up in the heart of a child, and it is not goodness of nature or whatever else you can talk of that will root it out, nor the rod of correction, unless the blood of the Lamb be sprinkled upon it" (199).

The sermons on Revelation 13 thus prove to be far more interesting and important than might have been supposed. From them we learn how it was that the Massachusetts Bay colonists could conceive of their efforts—strenuous but in the context of history microscopic—as a crucial part of God's magnificent plan. Congregationalism was to them the last step in the Reformation; its limited following was only an indication that it lacked the appeal of corrupt religion.

V   The Pouring Out of the Seven Vials

Cotton's interpretation of the prophecies of the Book of Revelation is only an incidental part of his commentary on the thirteenth chapter, but interpretation of prophecies is more important in *The Powrring out of the Seven Vials: or, An Exposition of the Sixteenth Chapter of the Revelation, with an Application of it to our Times*. These weekday lectures were published in 1645, presumably soon after they were delivered.

Cotton believed that he was living in a time when God was pouring out his wrath on everything Roman Catholic. God's angels had poured out a vial of wrath on the lowest and basest sort of Catholics because of their "damnable ignorance, and superstition, idolatry, and hypocrisy" (13); and the instruments of God's wrath were the forces of reformation in the time of

Henry VIII, Edward VI, and Mary. Then the worship and the religious practices of Roman Catholicism were attacked by English and Continental theologians: William Ames, William Perkins, Whitaker, and Junius.

Attacks on Roman Catholicism, with what Cotton conceives to be its hypocrisy, lead Cotton to a warning to New Englanders, whose religious principles are so pure that they are particularly susceptible to hypocrisy. He warns

all professors [all who profess Christianity] in this country and church members . . . all that profess they came out of England for purity of ordinances, to be very circumspect, pure, and faithful, and zealous in all their whole conversation, for believe it, you will find this true and remember it while you live, if you be corrupt in New England, if you be unfaithful here, if you be worldly-minded here, false of your words and promises here, injurious in your dealings here, believe it, one of these two will unavoidably follow: either all England will judge your reformation but a delusion and an invention of your magistrates or elders, or otherwise look at you as not sincere but counterfeit (21).

The eyes of England are on New England, Cotton still hopefully supposes.

Cotton also describes how God has been wrathful to the Catholic clergy, to the House of Austria, and to the Pope's supremacy. Now the remaining three vials are to be poured out. The destruction of episcopacy has for some time been in progress through the efforts of Thomas Cartwright and Calvin's successor, Theodore Beza; and now the work is continued through the Church of Scotland, busy fighting the Bishops' Wars. All of the efforts made to retain and reinforce episcopacy are, Cotton observes, prophesied to occur after the pouring out of the vial against episcopacy: "They repented not of their deeds." The attack on episcopacy will spread, Cotton foresees, to all Catholic countries.

The sixth vial signifies the attack on the supporters of Roman Catholicism, such as the Turks. The unclean spirits of Revelation 16:13 Cotton understands to be the cardinals, bishops and Jesuits, who croak "not like these frogs here in America that have a several tune in each part of the year . . ." (106).

This work ends with an extended description of the pouring out of the seventh vial and the consequent battle of Armageddon and the destruction of all iniquity. All these will occur before long, acording to Cotton. What a great time to be a Massachusetts Bay Congregationalist!

VI The Church's Resurrection

The optimism of this work is extended and modified in the single sermon on Revelation 20:5-6, *The Churches Resurrection*, published in 1642, presumably about the time it was delivered. In it Cotton pictures the millennium, which he believes is about to begin. It is a time of general spiritual awakening, to be followed by a long period when God will neglect those whom He has not called and their descendants. The time is crucial: ". . . if we do not now strike a fast covenant with our God to be His people, if we do not now abandon whatsoever savors of death in the world, of death in lust and passion, then we and ours will be of this dead-hearted frame a thousand years; we are not like to see greater encouragements for a good while than now we see" (16).

The signs of the church's resurrection, which Cotton sees abroad in England and Scotland, lead him to be most hopeful; but he sees all about him at home signs of degeneration. Many in New England are ready to return to England or to go west where there are no churches. Cotton warns his hearers that they can have no part in the resurrection if they say, "we could have large elbow room enough, and meadow enough, though we had no ordinances . . ." (26).

Cotton's millennial prophecies and hopes were shared by many in England. His prediction of a spiritual resurrection calls to mind Milton's picture of "a noble and puissant nation rousing herself like a strong man after sleep," a prophecy made in 1644, only two years after the publication of Cotton's sermon. The hopefulness of Milton's *Areopagitica* helps us to understand Cotton's optimism; and the parallel can be extended. Cotton's dedication of his life to the cause of further reformation makes one suspect that by the time of his death he had experienced enough defeats to make his feelings of frustration and disappointment quite comparable to Milton's.

VII   The Covenant of God's Free Grace

To some degree Cotton's own policies led to the failure of the New England Way. Perhaps the best indication of his tendency to tribalism, an important cause of the decay of Puritanism in America, is the sermon entitled *The Covenant of Gods Free Grace*. It may well be the most mature of Cotton's sermons—it was published in 1645, probably soon after it was delivered. The late date is suggested by its theme: that God will accept a man though his household be sinful. It was about the middle of the 1640's when the Congregationalists who had come to America from England discovered that their children were not able to qualify for church membership by testifying as to their faith. The sermon is then another testimony to Cotton's disappointment in what was to have been God's own commonwealth.

Cotton used as his text II Samuel 23:5: "Although my house be not so with God, yet He hath made with me an everlasting covenant, ordered in all things, and sure; for this is all my salvation, and all my desire, although He make it not to grow." Cotton tries to be hopeful, but at the same time he shows an awareness of an undesirable situation. God has "a secret purpose and counsel . . . to have some unbelievers in every family . . ." (6). Still he would not have church members despair, for they can help their families to amend. (Earlier he would have argued that such amendment of life meant simply reliance on a Covenant of Works.)

The most surprising aspect of this book is its explanation of how one can join himself to the covenantal relationship. To be within the covenant meant receiving federal or common grace, Cotton had taught in his treatise on baptism. Now the means which Cotton suggests is a demonstration of the tribalism which Edmund Morgan has suggested was a growing weakness of American Puritanism.[5] Cotton first suggests the study of genealogy: if any of a man's ancestors have been under the Covenant of Grace and he himself has not renounced it, he can consider that the Covenant reaches to him. If not, he can claim the Covenant if he has lived in a household within the Covenant. If he cannot qualify by either of these two approaches, he can still enter a household within the Covenant and wait on God for a deliverance. Gone is Cotton's evangelism; God's ways are better understood now.

Presumably those who enter the covenantal relationship by one of these methods can expect federal grace and thereby become likely candidates for saving grace. But, as Morgan observes in his discussion of the sermon, "the ministers did their best to make it difficult for an unregenerate man to enter a godly family" (*The Puritan Family*, 101). As a consequence of the belief that grace is most likely to come to those within the covenant and to their descendants, Puritanism in time became "hopelessly inbred"; for the Puritans had "lost their concern for the gospel of Christ in a smug assurance that their children would inherit grace" (*The Puritan Family*, 104).

We have none of Cotton's last sermons, where we might see if he ever spoke with evangelistic hope to the unregenerate members of his congregation.

In his own day Cotton was regarded as a great preacher, as is evidenced by the care taken by his many admirers in both Englands to print his sermons. Apparently, however, much of Cotton's appeal was in his personality. Very little of Cotton the man comes through to the reader of his sermons, though one can detect in them certain of his interests. He delighted in unraveling difficult passages in Scripture. (In 1636 Hugh Peter preached a sermon before Cotton's congregation in which he asked that Cotton be spared for a time "that he might go through the Bible, and raise marginal notes upon all the knotty places of Scripture"—Winthrop, *Journal* [1908], I, 179). He was deeply interested in the place of Congregationalism in Christian history. But most of his interests he shared with practically all other Puritan preachers: the salvation process, the need for those who think they are Christians to examine themselves continually, the omnipresence of death, a carefully restrained delight in God and in Jesus Christ, a sense of the passing of time, the need to devote oneself to one's vocation, a hatred of Roman Catholicism and the remains of it in the Church of England, the total depravity of natural man and his inability to improve his own spiritual condition, biblical history and the history of the early church, the use of the means of grace. Certain themes common to other Puritan preachers are notably absent from Cotton's sermons: denunciation of particular sins, concern for the relationship of husband and wife, the nature of God and His relation to the universe. Like most Puritans, Cotton shows little interest in the human life of Jesus.

What Cotton lacks most is vividness. His American colleagues Thomas Hooker and Thomas Shepard were more severe though less orthodox: but they were far more vigorous. Lawrence Sasek has made this generalization about the Puritan preacher: "Whatever his theory of style might exclude, concreteness and the imagery of everyday life, with their immediacy and strength of effect, had to be part of his repertory."[6] They were not in fact part of John Cotton's. The similitudes which William Haller finds to be one of the most popular features of the Puritan sermon are rare indeed with Cotton, unless he develops one already found in his text, like the one we have noted in *Gods Mercie Mixed with his Iustice*. "Illustrations of doctrine," says Haller, "drawn from everyday life, especially when touched with something like the interest of narrative, plainly took with the people" (*The Rise of Puritanism* [1958], 148). But Cotton's congregation could have no such pleasures.

The effectiveness of Cotton's preaching is beyond dispute. We have the testimony of John Winthrop that in 1633 "more were converted and added to that church [Cotton's] than to all the other churches in the Bay. . . . Divers profane and notorious evil persons came and confessed their sins, and were comfortably received into the bosom of the church" (*Journal*, I, 116). The lectures which supplemented the Sunday sermons were preached by popular demand; they could be heard by those who belonged to other churches, where they were expected to worship on Sundays.

But we have only Cotton's words, not the power of his presence. Let us compare a passage from Cotton's Salem sermon of 1636, an example of his usual style, with a passage from Peter Sterry, a Puritan contemporary of Cotton's.

Cotton:

> Now then, doth the Lord draw you to Christ when you are broken, in the sense of your own sins and of your own righteousness? When you look at duties you are not able to do them, not able to hear or pray aright. If the Lord do thus draw you by His everlasting arm, He will put a Spirit into you that will

cause you to wait for Christ and to wait for Him until He doth show mercy upon you; and if you may but find mercy at the last, you will be quiet and contented with it (32).

Sterry:

The truths which I am to believe lie in Scripture, as colors in the wall or in a picture. The Spirit is, as the light. I see the colored wall by the light, for that enlightens it, accentuates its shape and colors, brings them, unites them to my eye, enlightening and actuating that also. I see the light by the wall, for it reflects and directs itself from that to my eye. So the Spirit and the Scriptures, as light and colors on a picture are mutually seen in and by one another, without any maze or endless circle (*The Teaching of Christ in the Soule* [1648], 33).

The freshness of Sterry's analogy, the simplicity of the style, the sense of the person behind the prose all commend this passage. All of these characteristics are missing from the Cotton passage. Cotton is clear enough, but the style is in no way distinguished, unless one finds in it a comforting kindness, an attractive gentleness.

Cotton's sermons have far more to say to the historian than to the student of literary art. Despite occasional vivid passages, the sermons surely would have little literary interest were it not for his having been claimed for American literature. Cotton's best prose is elsewhere, in his works on Congregationalism, for here he felt none of the restraint of the Puritan pulpit pattern, the endless quoting of Scripture, the tiresome *thirdly's* and *fourthly's*.

CHAPTER 6

Defender of the Faith:
The Theological Writings

JOHN COTTON'S Puritanism cut him off from whatever sense of an Anglican tradition there was by the early seventeenth century. But it helped him to identify himself with what appeared to be more important: the Reformed tradition. Though frequently identified with Calvin and consequently often labeled Calvinist, the term "Reformed" embraces many theologians, Calvin (1509-64) being indeed foremost.

Two Continental writers of special importance for England were Martin Bucer (1491-1551) and Heinrich Bullinger (1504-75). Bucer, who anticipated Calvin's views on predestination, was regius professor of divinity at Cambridge University from 1549 to 1551; as late as 1595 English theologians acknowledged their indebtedness to him. Particularly significant was his interest in the salvation process, a subject which came to dominate much of Puritan thinking. Bullinger's influence was felt especially during the reign of the Catholic Mary (1553-58), for many English exiles lived in Zurich, where he taught. The large collection of his sermons, entitled *The Decades,* was all but accepted as official doctrine by the Church of England.

The influence of Calvin himself was immense. In Elizabethan England and into the seventeenth century, Calvin's *Institutes,* his biblical commentaries, and his sermons were translated and published time and again. His teachings were accepted by bishops and by non-conforming Puritans alike. His influence was especially great because his *Institutes* offered a systematic theology to replace those of the Catholic Schoolmen and because, before the time of Richard Hooker, there was no native Protestant theologian of much importance.

Yet the influence of Calvin can be easily misunderstood. Those doctrines usually identified with his name—the concepts that Christ died only for the elect, and that God's grace is irresistible—were not of much influence in the first half of Elizabeth's reign. Instead, in most Elizabethan sermons one finds what is historically thought of as Augustinianism, the doctrine that salvation comes through grace. It is this theology which dominates Alexander Nowell's semi-official catechism, Calvin's own catechism (adopted for use at both Oxford and Cambridge), and, most significantly, the official Thirty-Nine Articles, which were thoroughly acceptable both to Puritans and to supporters of the established Church.

The longest of the Articles is Number XVII, "Of Predestination and Election." It summarizes skillfully the Reformed doctrine of the day:

> Predestination to life is the everlasting purpose of God, whereby (before the foundations of the world were laid) He hath constantly decreed by His counsel secret to us, to deliver from curse and damnation those whom He hath chosen in Christ out of mankind, and to bring them by Christ to everlasting salvation, as vessels made to honor. Wherefore, they which be endued with so excellent a benefit of God, be called according to God's purpose by His Spirit working in due season: they through grace obey the calling; they be justified freely; they be made sons of God by adoption; they be made like the image of His only-begotten Son Jesus Christ; they walk religiously in good works; and at length, by God's mercy, they attain to everlasting felicity.

This article explains, as Calvin had, that the doctrine of election offers "to godly persons" the comfort of assurance of salvation.

The articles on original sin, free will, justification, and good works are consistent with Article XVII. In general, the Articles can be said to teach predestination, but not reprobation, and to emphasize God's grace.

These Articles date from 1563, the year before Calvin's death. During the latter part of the century a dominant figure was Calvin's successor, Theodore Beza, who spelled out the logical implications of the kind of doctrine found in Article XVII. He emphasized double predestination: election to salvation and reprobation to damnation. He marks the beginning of Protestant scholasticism, and Bezaism won victory after victory over less strict varieties of Reformed thought. The consequence was that Reformed orthodoxy reached such a point of refinement that Calvin himself "would probably have made a difficulty about adopting precise and definite deliverances on some points concerning the truth of which the great Calvinistic divines of the seventeenth century had no hesitation."[1]

English theology was inevitably affected by these changes. Some theologians rebelled and adopted positions later to be called Arminian. Most fully accepted the new doctrines. The best indication of their acceptance is the Lambeth Articles of 1595, which Thomas Fuller, a knowledgeable seventeenth-century church historian, tells us contain "the general and received doctrine of England in that age."[2] The nine articles are all brief:

1. God from eternity hath predestined certain men unto life; certain men He hath reprobated.
2. The moving or efficient cause of predestination unto life is not the foresight of faith, or of perseverance, or of good works, or of anything that is in the persons predestinated, but only the good will and pleasure of God.
3. There is predetermined a certain number of the predestinate, which can neither be augmented nor diminished.
4. Those who are not predestinated shall be necessarily damned for their sins.
5. A true, living, and justifying faith, and the Spirit of God justifying is not extinguished, falleth not away; it vanisheth not away in the elect, either finally or totally.
6. A man truly faithful, that is, such a one who is endued with a justifying faith, is certain, with the full assurance of faith, of the remission of his sins and of his everlasting salvation by Christ.
7. Saving grace is not given, is not granted, is not communicated to all men by which they may be saved if they will.
8. No man can come unto Christ unless it shall be given unto him, and unless the Father shall draw him; and all men are not drawn by the Father, that they may come to the Son.
9. It is not in the will or power of everyone to be saved.

With this increased theological sophistication concerning the salvation process came more intense study of the psychological aspects of conversion. William Perkins (1558-1602), whose preaching helped prepare Cotton for conversion, was an authority not only in the new High Calvinist theology but also in the new "experimental" theology. In his *A Treatise tending unto a declaration whether a man be in the estate of damnation or in the estate of grace,* Perkins was especially concerned with the question of how far a reprobate can go down the path to salvation and of how far a saint must go before he can be considered saved. Determining one's spiritual health was no longer an easy matter, as it had been for Calvin.

In his very important *A golden Chaine* (1600) Perkins combined his psychological with his theological interests. In it he explains, for example, how the reprobates are damned: "First, they have by nature ignorance and vanity of mind. After that followeth hardness of heart, whereby they become void of all sorrow for their sins. Then cometh a reprobate sense, which is when the natural light of reason and of the judgment of good and evil is extinguished. Afterward when the heart ceaseth to sorrow, then ariseth a committing of sin with greediness. Then cometh pollution, which is the fullness of sin. Lastly, a just reward is given to all these, to wit, fearful condemnation" (167).

I A Treatise of Predestination

Cotton discovered early in his career that the position of Perkins was doubly difficult for him. First, Cotton found the doctrine of reprobation a difficult one to treat in a sermon. In the sixteenth-century climate of opinion, a Protestant preacher had not been expected to preach strict predestinarian doctrine though more than likely his theological position was thoroughly Calvinistic. But by Cotton's day, with the new emphasis on the decrees of God, Cotton could not avoid the issue. Second, he discovered that, in the part of Lincolnshire where he was preaching, the semi-Pelagian theology of Arminius—the position popularly called Lutheranism—was attracting many followers. Arminius conceived of the salvation process as a cooperative one, with God *and* man each having a role. Cotton formulated a compromise doctrine, which might satisfy both followers of the Reformed position and those who had espoused the "Lutheran" position. In 1618, Cotton set forth his views in writing for the benefit of a neighboring minister, and this work then circulated in manuscript for many years. In 1633 William Twisse, a

Perkinsian theologian, had the opportunity to read the work and to prepare a refutation, which Cotton saw before he left that year for New England. In 1646 Cotton's treatise with Twisse's reply found its way into print. Thus *A Treatise of Mr. Cottons, Clearing certaine Doubts concerning Predestination. Together with an Examination Thereof: written by William Twisse, D.D.*, perhaps Cotton's earliest extant work, was finally published.

In his *Treatise* Cotton argues that God intended to glorify Himself before He presupposed that man would fall into sin. Christ was not created for us, that He might save the elect; we were created for Christ and God's glory. The decree of predestination has as its purpose the demonstration of God's justice and His grace, not His sovereignty, freedom, and dominion. Reprobation Cotton prefers to consider non-election, and its cause is God's foreknowledge of the sins of the reprobate, or at least of some of the reprobates.

The ingenuity of Cotton's scheme is worth demonstrating, for it shows the extent to which his personal feelings were apt to color his thinking. Cotton argues that God offers salvation to all the world on the conditions of obedience and repentance. Those ignorant of this offer sin nonetheless, because they sin against the law of nature in their hearts. The elect are forcibly changed by grace; the non-elect are strongly encouraged to change. "God giveth to the men of this world, I say, as opposed to the elect, such means and helps of seeking after the Lord and finding mercy from Him that they are sufficiently enabled by Him to do more than they do; that way they are deprived of those drawing and effectual means without which none can come to faith and repentance" (207). Note that Cotton does not declare that the non-elect *can* save themselves; their damnation is based seemingly on their failure to do what they can do. "Because of the abuse of these talents and means of grace God therefore doth deny to the men of this world such powerful and gracious helps as He vouchsafeth freely to the elect to draw them effectually to repentance and salvation" (241). The non-elect cannot obtain faith without grace; abuse of the means of grace presumably means failure to obtain faith through hearing sermons. But such a failure, such an abuse of the means, is altogether inevitable for those whom God has not chosen.

Though Cotton is said to have become persuaded that Twisse

was right, later he took his old position in his treatise on baptism and in his sermons on the Covenant of Grace. Yet in his New England years he argued, with Calvin, against voluntarism. Even in this *Treatise* he did not fail to identify himself with his tradition: "In the doctrine of election," he wrote, "I consent wholly with Augustine, Calvin, Beza, Martyr, Zanchy, Perkins, Paraeus, and others" (39). Cotton's departure from orthodoxy was, significantly, for the purpose of harmony among people. Cotton was primarily a preacher: his unhappiness with the dogma of reprobation was that it seemed to affect adversely his dealings with his people.

II A Treatise

After his arrival in the New World, Cotton soon found himself in the position of spokesman for the Puritan Commonwealth which was being established there. Some of the earliest documents which he prepared as spokesman were published in 1713 as *A Treatise*. Since at this time (1634) Cotton was attempting to set down the fundamental Christian doctrines as he conceived of them, the slimness of the work belies its importance. These twelve doctrines are taken for granted in most of Cotton's other works; for, as he writes here, if one denies these doctrines, he must be considered a heretic, though one or two admonitions should precede the denunciation. The twelve are:

1. God is in three persons, Father, Son, and Holy Ghost.
2. God made and governs the world; He rewards the good and punishes the evil.
3. Only God is to be worshiped.
4. The worship of God is to be performed "according to His written Word" (5).
5. Man is a sinful being and therefore a cursed one.
6. Man cannot rescue himself from this sinful state.
7. The Son became incarnate and, by perfect obedience to God, has redeemed His church.
8. Salvation is given to believers, and no man can believe except by being drawn to God.
9. "Those whom the Lord draws by His Word and Spirit to believe on Christ, them He justifies freely by His grace in Christ" (8).

10. Regeneration of the justified then follows.
11. But this regeneration is imperfect.
12. On Judgment Day men shall be judged by their works.

Prefaced to this summary is a definition of faith that makes more explicit certain of these doctrines. Cotton defines faith as a work of God "wrought by the ministry of the Word," whereby confidence in the flesh is abandoned and belief in God and His Son replace this false confidence. Cotton says nothing here about predestination, but it is implied by the seventh and eighth points, for the seventh limits the atonement to the elect, and the eighth limits the faithful to God's chosen.

This summary of Cotton's theological position indicates clearly that whereas the central events in human history are the Incarnation and the Atonement, the central event in the life of the believer is his being called to belief through the preaching of the Word. The minister's chief function is to preach, and as a preacher the minister is the most important man in a theocracy such as the Massachusetts Bay Colony.

III *The Case of Anne Hutchinson*

Much more sophisticated are Cotton's theological works written during the Antinomian crisis of 1636-37. These contrast sharply with the voluntarism seen in the treatise on predestination. They argue vigorously that man is wholly passive in the salvation process, which is God's work and not man's. Saving faith is a consequence of grace, of the union of the elect and Christ Jesus.

The case of Anne Hutchinson has usually been looked at as a revelation of the bigotry and narrow-mindedness of the Puritans and of the moral cowardice of John Cotton. Thanks to the studies of Emery Battis and Edmund Morgan,[3] we now see that Mrs. Hutchinson and her followers did present a threat to the unity and to the structure of the Massachusetts Bay Colony and that John Cotton was less a coward than a somewhat naïve, unworldly scholar. The Calvinism of Cotton's treatises produced during the controversy has been available for all to see, but they have been largely ignored.

Actually, the Anne Hutchinson episode loomed much larger in Cotton's career than it does in his works. Six titles deal with the matter, but the pamphlets *Sixteene Questions of Serious and Necessary Consequence* (1644) and *Severall Questions of Serious and Necessary Consequence* (1647) prove to be the same work, and so do the pamphlets *A Conference of Mr. John Cotton Held at Boston* (1646) and *Gospel Conversion* (1646). To understand these two pamphlets, one must consider the story of Cotton's dealings with Mrs. Hutchinson. Cotton tells the tale in *The Way of Congregational Churches Cleared* (1648), an answer to Robert Baillie's personal attack in *A Dissuasive from the Errours of our Time* (1645). The matter also comes up in the debate with Roger Williams; Cotton has some important remarks in "A Reply to Mr. Williams his Examination," which is part of *The Bloudy Tenent Washed* (1647).

Anne Hutchinson had lived in her early years twenty-four miles from Boston in Lincolnshire, England, in the town of Alford. The daughter of a strong-minded minister, Anne seems to have felt the need, from childhood, for external guidance. She did not obtain it from the man she married; indeed, she seemed to be a more domineering personality by far than her rather meek but industrious husband. In time she found the guidance she needed from John Cotton, whose sermons she heard with considerable frequency. The religious guidance which he provided was supplemented in time by the preaching of John Wheelwright, who had married the sister of Anne's husband and who lived within a mile of Alford. But even more comforting was the guidance which she came to feel in meditation, for here she felt God's presence.

In 1632, however, Wheelwright was removed from his position of minister, and in 1633 Cotton left for America. Unable to sustain these losses, Anne Hutchinson saw that she must go to America too. The fall of 1634 saw Anne, her husband, and her twelve children all in Boston. Here she put into use skills learned in England, and she soon was known and admired throughout the town as a helpful nurse and competent midwife. It is at this point that Cotton begins his story in *The Way . . . Cleared;* the narrative is quite consistent with all of the other evidence concerning what happened.

Cotton tells us that he had good reports of the work Mrs. Hutchinson did. He was pleased that she was concerned with the spiritual as well as with the physical state of the women she visited. Her special concern was to teach people not to depend on their works for their justification; she emphasized that the Covenant of Works brought with it graces which might appear to be saving but were dangerously deceptive. Since Cotton warns of the same danger in the published sermons in *A Treatise of the Covenant of Grace*, she was only following his teachings. In time she extended her efforts by reviewing Cotton's preached sermons with women of the congregation, and some men too. These efforts seemed to Cotton very proper and helpful: "these private conferences did well to water the seeds publicly sown" (51).

Eventually she extended the conferences to include summaries of what other ministers preached. (Though Cotton does not tell us, we know that John Wilson, Cotton's colleague of the church in Boston, was much disliked by Mrs. Hutchinson.) But since she did not repeat what she did not approve, she in fact became a critic of the local ministers. What she disapproved most was their way of recommending sanctification as a test of justification. Since she thought that those under a Covenant of Works were likely to detect some signs of sanctification in themselves, she rejected this test. Cotton himself had taught that sanctification was proof, but now he recognized that an emphasis on works left too much to man and man's own abilities.

Cotton was not wholly happy with Mrs. Hutchinson, even when she was not yet recognized as a source of heresy and discord. He warned her, he tells us, that she was prone to three errors: she trusted too much in "private meditations or revelations only" (52), she was unable to discern her sanctification as well as her justification, and she was too severe in her judgment of the spiritual condition of others.

As time went on, word got to ministers outside Boston about what Mrs. Hutchinson was doing. A group of them went to Cotton to report what was happening; they told him that Mrs. Hutchinson and her followers were spreading heresies. But when Cotton charged the Hutchinsonians with teaching errors, they denied that they taught what was charged against them. After further counsel with the clergy, Cotton decided to attack the

Hutchinsonians' teaching from his pulpit. But here too he got nowhere, for Mrs. Hutchinson's followers told those out of sympathy with them that "No matter . . . what you hear him say in public; we know what he saith to us in private" (40).

Although Cotton does not tell us of the matter himself, his teachings were the cause of much of the trouble. He did in fact differ from his colleagues in the ministry. The difference was small but it had significant implications: it made his preaching techniques basically different from those of his colleagues, especially those of his fellow minister in the Boston church, John Wilson. Doubtless both were at heart Calvinists; doubtless both taught that man can do nothing to save himself, but that grace must do all. The point where they differed was the question of proof. For Wilson, the proof that one had been given saving grace was his ability to do good works. For Cotton, the first evidence of grace was an awareness that the Spirit dwelt within one, the Spirit which illuminated and drew one to God. Sanctification is an effect of this indwelling of the Spirit, as is faith; but these are not at first as discernible as the sense of the Spirit's presence.

Cotton carefully qualified his views; Mrs. Hutchinson started with these same doctrines, but so emphasized the importance of the indwelling Spirit that she encouraged Quietism, which Puritanism always regarded as a great danger. Puritans called it familism, for they identified it with a Quaker-like sect known as the Family of Love. This emphasis on the indwelling Spirit promoted individualism, dangerous because it led to heresy. It also encouraged indolence, mere passive waiting. Moreover, it went against one of the underlying concepts of the Colony, one growing in importance: that the social covenant would bring blessings on the people if they walked in the way of godliness.

The threat of Mrs. Hutchinson's teachings was especially an attack on what has been called the organicism of the Bay Colony. Winthrop, in his "Model of Christian Charity," had described the personal relationships which were to develop in the Colony in this fashion:

> We must entertain each other in brotherly affection; we must be willing to abridge ourselves of our superfluities for the supply of others' necessities; we must uphold a familiar commerce together in all meekness, gentleness, patience, and liberality; we

must delight in each other; make others' conditions our own; rejoice together, mourn together, labor and suffer together, always having before our eyes our commission and community in the work, our community as members of the same body. So shall we keep the unity of the Spirit in the bond of peace. The Lord will be our God and delight to dwell among us as His own people and will command a blessing upon us in all our ways, so that we shall see much more of His wisdom, power, goodness, and truth than formerly we have been acquainted with. We shall find that the God of Israel is among us.[4]

Mrs. Hutchinson's ideas went against this much-desired unity. They even splintered into two factions the membership of the Boston church.

How much out of keeping with this program and its concept of the covenant Mrs. Hutchinson's teaching was may be suggested by the journal entry of a member of the Boston church. Winthrop wrote: "One Mrs. Hutchinson, a member of the church of Boston, a woman of a ready wit and bold spirit, brought over with her two dangerous errors: 1. That the person of the Holy Ghost dwells in a justified person. 2. That no sanctification can help to evidence to us our justification.—From these two grew many branches, as: 1. Our union with the Holy Ghost so as a Christian remains dead to every spiritual action and hath no gifts nor graces other than such as are in hypocrites, nor any other sanctification but the Holy Ghost Himself" (*Journal* [1908], I, 195-96).

IV   Sixteen Questions

Though Cotton did not know it, the ministers of the Colony continued to be concerned about the evil effects of Mrs. Hutchinson's teaching, especially since members of other churches were becoming advocates of the Boston troublemaker. When they arranged for a private conference with her, they discovered that she aligned herself with Cotton and considered the other ministers to be advocates of a decidedly different position. It was now Cotton's turn to be investigated. The questions he was asked and his answers constitute the little book *Sixteene Questions*.

The first five questions concern an expression that Mrs. Hutchinson had used, "the seal of the Spirit." This term Cotton conceives to be the witness of the Spirit. Without this witness a man cannot take comfort that he is saved: "The testimony of the Spirit is so clear as that it may witness immediately, though not without some work of Christ in a man, yet without respect unto the work. Nevertheless it is not so constant or permanent (at least not in all believers) but that a man after he hath received it may come in time of temptation to question his estate, though not so frequently nor so desperately as before" (6).

The next eight questions deal mainly with the relationship of good works (or sanctification) and justification. Cotton argues that sins may make one less sure that he is saved (the Spirit "will not speak wonted peace and comfort to him"), yet he will still feel assured even if he becomes degenerate. This position went against the teachings of most of Cotton's colleagues. The discernment of one's sanctification is indeed, Cotton admitted, an evidence of salvation; but no real assurance is possible "till the Spirit of God doth witness from Christ God's thoughts of peace towards him" (8). To rely on the discernment of one's sanctification is "to go on in a Covenant of Works" (9).

The other questions are of a varied nature and in no way crucial. Clearly the fundamental question is whether using sanctification as evidence of salvation is to rely on a Covenant of Works. For this question, which he tells us was "exposed to greatest agitation and exception," Cotton provides an answer— one as long as the other fifteen together—to avoid "all suspicion of ambiguity and obscurity" (14). Cotton is willing for sanctification to be considered a concurrent sign of justification, but if one builds "his justifying faith upon such evidences, he shall . . . go aside to a Covenant of Works" (12). If one sees only "an evident change in himself from a profane and civil course to a sanctified conversation," he should not suppose that he has been given saving grace (9).

The difference between Cotton and his fellow ministers on nearly all of the matters discussed in Cotton's little book were great indeed. Thomas Hooker, for example, taught that a man who has been assured of his salvation loses assurance when he sins. "When Christians grow cold in prayer and careless in holy duties," warned Hooker, "the Lord taketh away the light of His favor, and He leaves those sluggish hearts to themselves. Nay, God is forced even against His will and mind, even for the good of those Christians, to take away the comfort of His presence, so that now they begin to think they never had grace. If the Lord did not thus, they would never mend their pace, nor quicken up themselves to any holy duties."5

As the ministers came to realize that Cotton did differ from them in important ways, they showed great concern to reconcile their differences, the most obvious way being to try to persuade Cotton to change his views. Winthrop tells us that at a meeting of the General Court, the Colony's legislature, John Wilson diagnosed the situation as extremely dangerous; he "laid the blame upon these new opinions risen up amongst us, which all the magistrates, except the governor [Henry Vane] and two others, did confirm, and all the ministers but two" (*Journal,* I, 204).

The other minister was John Wheelwright, the minister to whom Anne Hutchinson had been so much attracted in England. Wheelwright had arrived in the colonies in the summer of 1636, only six months before. Soon he took a prominent part in the dispute. In January, Cotton tells us in *The Way Cleared,* there was "a solemn fast kept in all the churches." At the Boston church Wheelwright preached.

Wheelwright taught the same doctrines that Cotton had been defending. Men should not rely on sanctification as an evidence of justification. But Wheelwright went further. He recognized that a difference of opinion existed and declared war on the adversaries, who were in fact most of the ministers of the Colony. "We must all of us prepare for battle," exhorted Wheelwright, "and come out against the enemies of the Lord; and if we do not strive, those under a Covenant of Works will prevail" (Adams, *Three Episodes,* I, 439).

In the preceding June, Cotton had preached at Salem that "Reformation is no assurance that God hath made an everlasting Covenant with us" (*A Sermon . . . Deliver'd at Salem, 1636* [1713], 31). But Wheelwright's sermon was received not as a doctrinal teaching but as a battle cry. Winthrop was much distressed that Wheelwright should call those who "maintain sanctification as an evidence of justification, etc.," "Antichrists" (*Journal,* I, 211). He noted that ". . . Mr. Wheelwright's sermon was apprehended to give too much encouragement to the opinionists [with whom Cotton did not identify himself]. And himself hath since confessed that, being but new come into the country, having but little acquaintance but with his kindred [who included Anne Hutchinson] and their friends (who were many of them leavened this way) he spake some things which, if he had before discerned their familism, he would not have expressed himself as he did" (*Way Cleared,* 40).

But Wheelwright knew to whom he was speaking. According to the studies of Emery Battis, 101 of the 169 members of the Boston church were supporters of Anne Hutchinson; seventy-three percent of the rich officeholders supported her. Although John Winthrop was firmly opposed, another important member of the Boston church, Henry Vane, was an enthusiastic disciple; and Vane was at this time governor of the Colony.

At this point Cotton took a position that reveals what he thought of his fellow ministers' theology and also how unwilling he was to become embroiled in debate. The General Court cited Wheelwright, far more vulnerable than Cotton, for sedition. He was asked whether in his sermon he had said that some of the Colony's ministers were under a Covenant of Works. His reply was that he had, if there were ministers who fit the description that he had provided. When all of the ministers except Cotton agreed that the shoe fit them, Wheelwright was found guilty. Cotton's comment on this is most illuminating:

> That I did not consent with the rest of my brethren (the elders) in drawing the inference out of Mr. Wheelwright's sermon, which they (being required) presented to the Court, I had a twofold reason for it. 1. Because I was not present with them when they searched Mr. Wheelwright's sermon and gathered that inference from it. [He had, however, heard it.] 2. Because I could not speak it of mine own knowledge. . . .
>
> . . . .
>
> They knew what themselves taught in that point better than I. The elders might testify what they knew; I could not testify what I knew not (*Way Cleared,* 59-60).

But the magistrates of the General Court had been told by the Bostonians that religious opinions were not their business, and, though they rejected this view of the matter, they felt it was up to the churches to label as heresies the teachings of the Hutchinsonians. The proper instrument was the synod, as John

Cotton himself taught; and in August, 1637, it was to begin. For it the ministers prepared a collection of all the questionable opinions that had been circulating and also a collection of Cotton's teachings which some ministers considered erroneous.

Identifying Cotton's questionable doctrines was preliminary to the synod because the ministers wanted to present a united front. They felt that, if they could show Cotton that his doctrines were different from those of all of the rest, they could then persuade him to abandon his teachings, or at least to compromise with them. But for some reason which is not known, the point of disagreement was not now what it had been throughout the controversy—the role of sanctification in determining the condition of the soul—but the role of faith in the conversion process. One of the *Sixteene Questions* had indeed concerned whether God's promises are absolute or conditional; now the heart of the matter seemed to be whether faith was a qualification for justification, or, to put it another way, whether faith is a cause of salvation. But on both points Cotton was the more consistent Calvinist.

To emphasize good works as proof of one's justification and to argue that a man's faith caused his justification required man to be active, not passive. The other ministers did not abandon at this time or later the High Calvinist theology which was to be formulated in the Westminster Confession, adopted by the Synod of 1648. But they wanted to exhort their people from the pulpit to believe because faith would lead to salvation. They used the sermon as a means of reconciling human responsibility and God's irresistible grace. Very likely the cause of the dispute with Cotton was that he chose to think in abstract, theological terms; they were concerned with the practical necessity of using an effective preaching technique.

The whole matter becomes clearer when we see the kind of teaching to be found in New England pulpits outside Boston. Thomas Shepard, preaching nearby at what is now Cambridge, taught that one of the reasons that God had made so many promises to His people was

> that His people might have a fit object for their faith to lay hold upon; for if you look upon all the creatures in the world, you shall not find in all of them jointly, or any of them apart a fit object for faith to work upon or be satisfied in. It is with faith

as with a poor woman that hath a child and hath nothing in the world to give it. She takes the child at her back and goeth from door to door, and what she getteth she giveth to the child. So faith takes the soul and carrieth it to promise after promise, and whatever she finds there, she gives it to the soul.

. . . .

Is it so, that God hath made many promises unto His people? Let us try ourselves, whether we have any right to the promises or no. I will name but one note that you may the better remember it, and it is a true one, for you shall find it in Scripture. "But the Scripture hath concluded all under sin that the promise by faith in Jesus Christ might be given to them that believe." So that you may see it is to them, and to them only, that believe. He that can exercise faith in the promise hath right to the promise. "For ye walk by faith and not by sight."[6]

Shepard also taught that man by nature cannot "speak one good word or do any good action if Heaven itself did lie at the stake for doing it."[7] The latter doctrine was wholly acceptable to Cotton, but not the former.

Thomas Hooker clarifies Shepard's meaning theologically in the following passage:

God is bound to none further than He will bind Himself; and He binds Himself in no wise to the creature but by His promise, and that He will never deny, Who cannot deny Himself. Now in the Gospel only this promise and engagement of God is revealed. He hath promised to work the condition [that is, to supply faith], and then tied Himself in His truth to do good to those whom He will so fit for His mercy. And now the soul upon this notice grows in upon God. Here is a handle, as it were, for faith to lay hold on. . . .[8]

As Hooker and Shepard describe the conversion process, the promises inspire faith, and faith is a possession of God's elect.

The preachers who hold forth the promises are in Hooker's words "co-workers with the Son"; together they "bring the poor creature and his Creator together."[9] The preacher's function is to be an expert psychologist who can "work upon the will and affections and by savory, powerful, and affectionate application of the truth delivered to chafe into the heart, to woo and win the soul to the love and liking, the approbation and practice of the doctrine which is according to godliness. . . ."[10] Hooker's and Shepard's concern was, then, to justify a technique but not to deny that salvation depends wholly on God's supplying the faith which saves. They wanted to be the Son's co-worker by helping men to find a handle to grasp salvation by.

Cotton insisted that union with Christ is complete *before* faith; indeed, the union is the cause of faith. In his 1636 Salem sermon he had preached: "If you come to Christ by virtue of anything which is in you, it is but a legal work" (32). He even denied what might have been a compromise: that, though union with Christ precedes faith, faith is experienced first. The presence of the Spirit Itself, he declared in *The Way Cleared,* is the first evidence that one has been called to salvation. In support of his teaching that faith is not the cause of salvation, Cotton quotes from Calvin that faith is "founded on the truth of a free promise in Christ," and that "this promise must be gratuitous; for a conditional promise, which throws us back upon our works, promises life only in so far as we find it existing in ourselves" (*Institutes,* III, ch. ii, sects. 7 and 29). Without a real agreement between Cotton and his colleagues, the synod then began.

Cotton did not consider his difference from the other ministers on these points to be a matter of great concern, but at the synod he was shocked to discover that members of his congregation were ready to defend doctrines which were generally considered heretical. He warned them that to defend these doctrines was to make "all these bastardly opinions, which are justly offensive to the churches" to "be fathered upon Boston" (*Way Cleared,* 47). But all of the Bostonians were not willing to condemn the doctrines, and some walked out of the synod to demonstrate their displeasure at what was happening. Now Cotton saw the light. But what struck him was his differences not with the other ministers but with his own parishioners: ". . . that (to my remembrance) was the first time of my discerning a real and broad difference between the judgments of our brethren (who leaned to Mistress Hutchinson) and myself." Realizing how dangerous it would be to be identified with the Hutchinsonians, Cotton quickly labeled "Some of the opinions to be blasphemous; some of them heretical; many of them erroneous, and almost all of them incommodiously expressed, as intending to except those chiefly wherein I had declared my own opinion, as before" (48).

V Gospel Conversion

In time the synod denounced all of the eighty-odd doctrines which had been collected; now the ministers were to try to settle their differences with Cotton. Eventually these were reduced to three. Cotton's views on them constitute the forty-eight pages of *Gospel Conversion* (1646). From the prefatory epistle it is clear that Cotton did not intend this work for publication, but its history is otherwise obscure. It is one of Cotton's most sophisticated theological works.

Question One is treated briefly. Cotton contends that there are no "gracious qualifications" in the soul *before* faith and no gracious qualifications before union with Christ. The fullest discussion is reserved for the second question, the matter that had begun the whole controversy: whether a man may evidence his justification by his sanctification. In his defense of over thirty pages Cotton cites many authorities, notably John Calvin and his own old critic William Twisse. But Cotton does not budge an inch from his position that sanctification is not a good evidence of justification: "I never read it," Cotton declares, "to my best remembrance in any author old or new that ever a man received his first evidence of the faith of his justification from his sanctification, unless it be one (whom I met within these two days) printed within these two years that maintaineth our first comfort of justification from sanctification. But generally all our English orthodox teachers do oppose it" (34-35).

The third question is "Whether faith concur as an active instrumental cause to our justification?" No, argues Cotton; "Faith may be said to be passive in our justification because it doth not lay hold on Christ to fetch justification from Him till Christ have first laid hold on us and imputed His righteousness to us and declared it unto us by His Spirit in a free promise of grace. And then faith becometh active . . ." (45).

The consequence of this extended doctrinal dispute is difficult to determine. Perry Miller says that in the end Cotton abjectly surrendered,[11] but Emery Battis sees the outcome quite different-ly: "Although subjected to humiliating pressures he was, in the last analysis, obliged to do little more than restate his original position in less equivocal terms."[12] Cotton's own comment, eleven years afterward, was that he was sorry that the dispute had ever taken place, that he was guilty for having permitted members of his church to disseminate errors without his detect-ing them, and "that such as endeavored the healing of these distempers did seem to me to be transported with more jealousies and heats and paroxysms of spirit than would well stand with brotherly love or the rule of the Gospel" (*Way Cleared*, 63). He does admit that in the settling of the dispute some truth was lost. In a letter he wrote to Samuel Stone on March 27, 1638, he confessed that he had made "a disorderly expression of the order and place of faith" at the meeting following the synod.[13] This letter confirms the hazy statement in *The Way Cleared* that he accepted some of the phraseology of the other ministers to settle the dispute.

Even after the synod Cotton was not fully persuaded that Mrs. Hutchinson was as wrong as the other ministers thought, perhaps because the doctrines for which she was ultimately condemned were to a large degree the product of Cotton's teach-ing. His emphasis on the soul's union with Christ in justification led her to think that she could because of this relationship have knowledge by direct revelation. When she was tried publicly, Cotton tried to help her without identifying himself with her opinions. But she was nevertheless sentenced to be banished. When she was examined in the Boston church to see whether she should be excommunicated, Cotton saw to it that her good works as well as her errors were brought to light. Only when she defended herself by maintaining that she had arrived at her errors after her public trial—a statement Cotton knew to be false—did he recognize that to try to defend her was hopeless. She was then excommunicated. Clearly Cotton had fulfilled his responsibilities to his parishioner.

The end of the story Cotton tells both in *The Way Cleared* and in the second part of *The Bloudy Tenent Washed*. His dealings with Mrs. Hutchinson had

> bred in sundry of the country a jealousy that I was in secret a
> fomenter of the spirit of familism, if not leavened myself that

way. Which I discerning, it wrought in me thoughts—as it did in many other sincerely godly brethren of our church—not of a separation from the churches as being legal (whom we truly embraced and honored in the Lord) but of a removal to New Haven, as being better known to the pastor [John Davenport] and some others there than to such as were at that time jealous of me here. The true ground whereof was an inward loathness to be troublesome to godly minds . . . (*Bloudy Tenent Washed,* Pt. II, p. 51).

But Winthrop and some of the other magistrates and ministers finally persuaded him to stay.

The two works of Cotton which resulted from the controversy are of no great importance except that they demonstrate not only the identity of Cotton's views with those of Calvin but also his willingness to stand behind unpopular theological opinions. Those who argue that the activist preaching of the New England Puritans shows them not to have been Calvinists should note Cotton's dependence, in his carefully marshaled arguments in the Anne Hutchinson controversy, on Calvin and such later High Calvinist theologians as his critic William Twisse.

VI   Milk for Babes

Cotton's most popular book was doubtless *Milk for Babes. Drawn Out of the Breasts of both Testaments. Chiefly, for the spirituall nourishment of Boston Babes in either England: But may be of like use for any Children* (1646). This catechism went through nine printings in the seventeenth century.

Milk for Babes is a remarkable document. It sums up with great succinctness Cotton's main interests as a teacher in words that a child could readily understand. Cotton's catechism deals with God, man, the Ten Commandments, Jesus Christ and His office, the plan of salvation, the church, the sacraments, and the Last Judgment. Each answer is accompanied by as many as eight Scriptural references. Today the work is rare indeed, and since without the references it is less than two thousand words in length, it is well worth reproducing here.

Q. What hath God done for you?
A. God hath made me, He keepeth me, and He can save me.
Q. Who is God?

A. God is a Spirit of Himself and for Himself.

Q. How many gods be there?
A. There is but one God in three persons, the Father, the Son, and the Holy Ghost.

Q. How did God make you?
A. In my first parents holy and righteous.

Q. Are you then born holy and righteous?
A. No, my first father sinned, and I in him.

Q. Are you then born a sinner?
A. I was conceived in sin and born in iniquity.

Q. What is your birth-sin?
A. Adam's sin imputed to me and a corrupt nature dwelling in me.

Q. What is your corrupt nature?
A. My corrupt nature is empty of grace, bent unto sin, and only unto sin, and that continually.

Q. What is sin?
A. Sin is the transgression of the Law.

Q. How many commandments of the Law be there?
A. Ten.

Q. What is the First Commandment?
A. Thou shalt have no other gods but me.

Q. What is the meaning of this commandment?
A. That we would worship the only true God and no other beside Him.

Q. What is the Second Commandment?
A. Thou shalt not make to thyself any graven image, &c.

Q. What is the meaning of this commandment?
A. That we should worship the true God with true worship such as God hath ordained, not such as man hath invented.

Q. What is the Third Commandment?
A. Thou shalt not take the name of the Lord thy God in vain, &c.

Q. What is here meant by the name of God?
A. God Himself and the good things of God, whereby He is known, as a man by his name, as His attributes, worship, Word, and works.

Q. What is it not to take His name in vain?
A. To make use of God and the good things of God to His

glory and our good, not vainly, not unreverently, not unprofitably.

Q. What is the Fourth Commandment?
A. Remember that thou keep holy the Sabbath day, &c.

Q. What is the meaning of this comandment?
A. That we should rest from labor and much more from play on the Lord's day, that we may draw nigh to God in holy duties.

Q. What is the Fifth Commandment?
A. Honor thy father and thy mother, that thy days may be long in the land which the Lord thy God giveth thee.

Q. Who are here meant by father and mother?
A. All our superiors, whether in family, school, church, and commonwealth.

Q. What is the honor due to them?
A. Reverence, obedience, and (when I am able) recompense.

Q. What is the Sixth Commandment?
A. Thou shalt do no murder.

Q. What is the meaning of this commandment?
A. That we should not shorten the life or health of ourselves or others but preserve both.

Q. What is the Seventh Commandment?
A. Thou shalt not commit adultery.

Q. What is the sin here forbidden?
A. To defile ourselves or others with unclean lusts.

Q. What is the duty here commanded?
A. Chastity, to possess our vessels in holiness and honor.

Q. What is the Eighth Commandment?
A. Thou shalt not steal.

Q. What is the stealth here forbidden?
A. To take away another man's goods without his leave, or to spend our own without benefit to ourselves or others.

Q. What is the duty here commanded?
A. To get our goods honestly, to keep them safely, and to spend them thriftily.

Q. What is the Ninth Commandment?
A. Thou shalt not bear false witness against thy neighbor.

Q. What is the sin here forbidden?

A. To lie falsely, to think or speak untruly of ourselves or others.

Q. What is the duty here required?
A. Truth and faithfulness.

Q. What is the Tenth Commandment?
A. Thou shalt not covet, &c.

Q. What is the coveting here forbidden?
A. Lust after the things of other men and want of contentment with our own.

Q. Whether have you kept all these commandments?
A. No, I and all men are sinners.

Q. What is the wages of sin?
A. Death and damnation.

Q. How look you then to be saved?
A. Only by Jesus Christ.

Q. Who is Jesus Christ?
A. The eternal Son of God, who for our sakes became man that He might redeem and save us.

Q. How doth Christ redeem and save us?
A. By His righteous life and bitter death and glorious resurrection to life again.

Q. How do we come to have part and fellowship with Christ in His death and resurrection?
A. By the power of His Word and Spirit, which bring us to Christ and keep us in Him.

Q. What is His Word?
A. The Holy Scriptures of the prophets and apostles, the Old and New Testament, Law and Gospel.

Q. How doth the ministry of the Law bring you towards Christ?
A. By bringing me to know my sin and the wrath of God against me for it.

Q. What are you thereby the nearer to Christ?
A. So I come to feel my cursed estate and need of a savior.

Q. How doth the ministry of the Gospel help you in this cursed estate?
A. By humbling me yet more and then raising me up out of this estate.

Q. How doth the ministry of the Gospel humble you more?
A. By revealing the grace of the Lord Jesus in dying to save

sinners and yet convincing me of my sin in not believing on Him and of mine utter insufficiency to come to Him, and so I feel myself utterly lost.

Q. How then doth the ministry of the Gospel raise you up out of this lost estate to come unto Christ?

A. By teaching me the value and the virtue of the death of Christ and the riches of His grace to lost sinners, by revealing the promise of grace to such and by ministering the Spirit of grace to apply Christ and His promise of grace unto myself and to keep me in Him.

Q. How doth the Spirit of grace apply Christ and His promise of grace unto you and keep you in Him?

A. By begetting in me faith to receive Him, prayer to call upon Him, repentance to mourn after Him, and new obedience to serve Him.

Q. What is faith?

A. Faith is a grace of the Spirit whereby I deny myself and believe on Christ for righteousness and salvation.

Q. What is prayer?

A. It is a calling upon God in the name of Christ by the help of the Holy Ghost, according to the will of God.

Q. What is repentance?

A. Repentance is a grace of the Spirit whereby I loath my sins and myself for them and confess them before the Lord and mourn after Christ for the pardon of them and for grace to serve Him in newness of life.

Q. What is newness of life or new obedience?

A. Newness of life is a grace of the Spirit whereby I forsake my former lusts and vain company, and walk before the Lord in the light of His Word and in the communion of His saints.

Q. What is the communion of saints?

A. It is the fellowship of the church in the blessings of the Covenant of Grace and the seals thereof.

Q. What is the church?

A. It is a congregation of saints joined together in the bond of the Covenant to worship the Lord and to edify one another in all His holy ordinances.

Q. What is the bond of the Covenant in which the church is joined together?

A. It is the profession of that Covenant which God hath made

with His faithful people to be a God unto them and to their
seed.

Q. What doth the Lord bind His people to in this Covenant?
A. To give up themselves and their seed first to the Lord to be
His people and then to the elders and brethren of the church
to set forward the worship of God and their mutual
edification.

Q. How do they give up themselves and their seed to the Lord?
A. By receiving, through faith, the Lord and His Covenant
to themselves and to their seed, and accordingly walking
themselves and training up their children in the ways of
His Covenant.

Q. How do they give up themselves and their seed to the elders
and brethren of the church?
A. By confession of their sins and profession of their faith and
of their subjection to the Gospel of Christ. And so they and
their seed are received into the fellowship of the church and
the seals thereof.

Q. What are the seals of the Covenant now in the days of the
Gospel?
A. Baptism and the Lord's Supper.

Q. What is done for you in baptism?
A. In baptism the washing with water is a sign and seal of my
washing with the blood and Spirit of Christ and thereby of
my ingrafting into Christ, of the pardon and cleansing of my
sins, of my rising up out of affliction, and also of my resurrection from the dead at the last day.

Q. What is done for you in the Lord's Supper?
A. In the Lord's Supper the receiving of the bread broken and
the wine poured out is a sign and seal of my receiving the
communion of the body of Christ broken for me, and of
His blood shed for me, and thereby of my growth in Christ,
of the pardon and healing of my sins, of the fellowship of
His Spirit, of my strengthening and quickening in grace,
and of my sitting together with Christ on His throne of
glory at the Last Judgment.

Q. What is the resurrection from the dead, which was sealed
up to you in baptism?
A. When Christ shall come to His Last Judgment, all that are in
the graves shall arise again, both the just and unjust.

Q. What is the Last Judgment which is sealed up to you in the Lord's Supper?

A. At the last day we shall all appear before the judgment seat of Christ to give an account of our works and to receive our reward according to them.

Q. What is the reward that shall then be given?

A. The righteous shall go into life eternal, and the wicked shall be cast into everlasting fire with the devil and his angels.

Despite this ominous ending, Cotton's *Milk for Babes* was not intended to terrify children; it emphasizes rather the orthodox theology on the one hand and strict morality on the other. Since it is strict morality which in the popular mind characterizes Puritanism, it is worth noting that, though Cotton's sermons are always serious, he seldom deals with the demands of morality in them. The catechism is a reminder that what were considered to be the duties of a Christian were taught nonetheless, and H. B. Parkes, who has studied the colonial records with care, reports that moral standards were in fact extraordinarily high.[14]

Cotton's expansion of the Ten Commandments is in keeping with his opinion that all principles of morality should be referred to the Commandments. Especially characteristic is his interpretation of the Second Commandment, which limits the ways of worship to what the Bible prescribes, a view which Cotton presents again and again in his writings. Cotton follows the influential teaching of William Ames on the scope of this commandment.[15] The restriction which Cotton finds in the Fourth Commandment, against play on the Lord's Day, is not only a reminder that his catechumen is a child but calls to mind that King James in old England had required ministers to declare from the pulpit the lawfulness of sports on the Sabbath.

Cotton's interpretation of the Fifth Commandment to demand that teachers, ministers, and magistrates be honored as well as parents seems at first to be one of the few reminders that the Bay Colony was an organic unit, with all parts considered to have an intimate interrelationship. But this idea is a Puritan commonplace, found, for example, in Perkins' *A golden Chaine.* Perhaps more enduring in New England has been the injunction to spend one's goods thriftily.

Cotton's teaching on the role of the preacher in the salvation process is less helpful than one expects as a guide to his sermon practice, for Cotton in his extant sermons does not stress the wrath of God, though he does teach that man on his own is unable to come to Jesus for redemption. But for a brief statement of church polity, the catechism is most helpful.

Its influence was great if not easy to state. Cotton Mather reports—in *Magnalia Christi Americana* (III, 28)—that at the turn of the century "The children of New England are to this day most usually fed with his excellent catechism, which is entitled *Milk for Babes.*" Since the law required all masters of families to catechize "their children and servants in the grounds and principles of religion,"[16] the book presumably was learned thoroughly by many a Massachusetts Bay child. In many ways *Milk for Babes* is the most accessible and attractive brief statement of the values of the first generation of American Puritans; it deserves to be better known.

Perhaps because he was a Congregationalist who valued the concept of the Covenant of Grace and yet was also a strict Calvinist of the mid-seventeenth-century variety, Cotton's theological works reveal strange inconsistencies. The works prepared when he was under pressure to abandon some of his High Calvinism are his most Calvinistic; as a preacher, he urged the validity of both voluntarism and spiritual inability. In his works on baptism and in his treatment of the children of the Covenant, he mixed his teachings painfully and paradoxically. In his catechism, where he could deal with elementary matters, he did manage to avoid knotty points. Church polity, not the doctrine of salvation, was Cotton's great interest. As a theologian he has little importance.

CHAPTER 7

Spokesman for Organicism:
The Controversy with Williams

JOHN COTTON is probably best known in American intellectual history for his debate with Roger Williams over religious toleration. In this debate, Cotton expressed opinions that have been called medieval, while Williams has usually been considered the apostle of enlightened modernism. Though Williams is doubtless the more attractive figure, Cotton's position in the debate is well worth considering, for it helps us to understand Cotton's view of the Massachusetts Bay Colony.

I *Williams in Massachusetts*

Roger Williams arrived in Boston in February, 1631, seven months after John Winthrop and the other leaders of the Bay Company and more than two and a half years before Cotton reached America.[1] During his time in Massachusetts before Cotton arrived, Williams managed to make a good many enemies and very few friends. First, he refused to be made teacher of the Boston church—the post later held by Cotton—and his refusal left the church with no minister at all for a time. His reason was that the church was not separated from the corruption of the Church of England. The colonists were ready to admit the truth of the charge, for they had never regarded themselves as Separatists, or like their Plymouth neighbors. Though Williams apparently came to New England to join his religious brethren, he refused even to join the Boston church. He also criticized the established government for permitting magistrates to punish religious offenses such as Sabbath breaking. In May he accepted the position of teacher of the church at Salem, which he soon left for the Separatism of Plymouth. There he served for a time as assistant minister and made himself unpopular with the authorities by preparing a treatise which branded as illegal the patent by which the king had granted land to the English. Williams was a gadfly whose admirable personal qualities were mixed with an uncomfortable iconoclasm.

Soon after John Cotton arrived in America, Williams returned to Salem. He had left Plymouth because its church was not pure enough: it did not excommunicate members who attended Church of England services during visits to England. At Salem he was again made teacher, and again he complained about the magistrates' punishing offenders against the first four of the Ten Commandments. He also taught that it was wrong for a magistrate to administer an oath to an unregenerate person. When Williams was called to give an accounting to the Massachusetts General Court, Cotton tried unsuccessfully to persuade him of his errors. The members of Williams' church at Salem began to show unhappiness with his views. When he demanded that the Salem church renounce communion with the other Bay Colony churches, the members refused, and he severed his relationship with the church. Williams demanded more of the church and less of the state than the Colony's program called for.

At a hearing given him by the Court in October, 1635, Williams defended his opinions, but there was no meeting of minds. He was given the opportunity to reconsider his attacks on the Colony and his own relationship to it and to its churches; the matter was then to be discussed again, a month later. But Williams refused the offer. When Thomas Hooker could not persuade Williams that he was wrong, he was ordered to leave the Colony within six weeks because he had defamed the magistrates and the churches and propagated opinions against the authority of the magistrates. When he continued to air his opinions, the magistrates decided to send him back to England on a ship about to depart. But before he could be taken, he fled—in the middle of the winter—to the area which was to be Rhode Island.

Cotton's role in these controversies with Williams was that of spokesman for the Massachusetts standing order. As a minister, he was free to deal with Williams more tactfully than the magistrates. Thomas Hooker played a similar part, but from later developments it appears that Williams considered Cotton as the chief spokesman for the Colony and as indeed the source of his problems.

II *Publication of the Debate*

To Williams in the Narragansett country Cotton addressed a letter, in which he tried once more to argue Williams out of his beliefs concerning the need for the New England churches to have absolute purity. This letter was later published at a time fortuitous for Williams, but he denied that he had it published. It is *A Letter of Mr. John Cottons to Mr. Williams* (1643). Williams published a reply the following year, *Mr. Cottons Letter Lately Printed, Examined and Answered* (1644).

At about the time of the preparation of his reply, Williams wrote another criticism of John Cotton. This time he answered a previously unpublished work of Cotton's, itself a reply to a letter from an English prisoner who had collected arguments opposed to religious intolerance. Williams published the letter, Cotton's reply, and his own reply to Cotton as *The Bloudy Tenent of Persecution, for Cause of Conscience, Discussed* (1644). The first two of these documents, without Williams' criticism, appeared two years later as *The Controversie Concerning Liberty of Conscience in Matters of Religion* (1646).

Why did Williams publish, years after his banishment, his two attacks on Cotton? For one thing, Williams was in England, where he had access to printing presses, though even in England *The Bloudy Tenent* had to be published surreptitiously. Second, the English Independents were seeking to attract to their cause against the Presbyterians the members of the various sects which had been rapidly developing. By showing that Cotton's New England Way was one of intolerance and persecution, Williams urged the sects not to identify themselves with the Congregational Independents.

In time Cotton replied to both of Williams' attacks. In the first part of *The Bloudy Tenent of Persecution, Washed and Made White in the Bloud of the Lambe* (1647) Cotton republished his views on toleration, Williams' reply (in *The*

Bloudy Tenent), and his own rejoinder. The second part is entitled "A Reply to Mr. Williams His Examination; and Answer of the Letters sent to him by John Cotton." The debate has three aspects: the purity of the New England churches, the justice of Williams' banishment, and the propriety of the Massachusetts policy of religious intolerance.

III The Issues

The root of the difference between the two ministers was the relationship of church and state. Cotton conceives of the two as cooperating powers: the state protects the church from disturbance, while the church selects the leaders of the state from among its members. He does not imagine that the church can be completely pure, though membership is carefully limited to those who appear to be saints. Since ministers are not elected to serve as political leaders, a kind of separation of church and state exists.

Williams, on the other hand, advocates a more radical separation and believes that genuine purity is possible in the church. His views are much less clear than Cotton's on the nature of the church, for—as he declared in *Queries of the Highest Consideration* (1644)—he was a Seeker who was dissatisfied with all known concepts of the church. (The Seekers believed that they must seek further light from God before they could determine which was the true church.) With this belief that truth was not known but was to be known, Williams was all but forced to become an advocate of tolerance.

Cotton insists that the New England churches are reformed churches, that their members have repented the practices they had prior to their establishing pure religion in America. What is needed, Cotton urges, is for church members to hate what separated them from Christ, not to denounce those Christians who have not yet rejected all impure practices. Thus ". . . we conceive the Lord hath guided us to walk with an even foot between two extremes; so that we neither defile ourselves with the remnant of pollutions in other churches, nor do we for the remnant of pollutions renounce the churches themselves, nor the holy ordinances of God amongst them, which ourselves have found powerful to our salvation. This moderation, so far as we have kept it in preaching or printing, we see no cause to repent of, but if you show us cause why we should repent of it, we shall desire to repent that we repented no sooner" (*A Letter of Mr. John Cottons*, 11).

Cotton charges that Williams' policies were too demanding; he had stopped "the bread of life from feeding hungry souls." Williams replies: "I would not, and the Lord Jesus would not, that one drop or one crumb or grain should be unlawfully, disorderly, or prodigally disposed of" (*Mr. Cottons Letter Lately Printed*, 8). Others accused the New England churches of demanding too much of their members; Roger Williams alone found them demanding too little.

Their disagreement about church membership eventually centered around their varied interpretations of the parable of the tares in Matthew 13. Cotton's Congregationalism held that church membership inevitably included hypocrites as well as saints. The tares in the parable he understands to be these hypocrites, who cannot be removed without plucking out some saints as well; for saints are like flowers "who sometimes lose their . . . sweetness for a season" (*Bloudy Tenent Washed*, Pt. I, p. 48). Cotton feared that the truth of the parable was demonstrated at the time of the Antinomian crisis, when excommunication might have eliminated both tares and wheat, hypocrites and saints.

Williams believes that it is possible to detect the hypocrites and that to permit them to remain within the church "is contrary to all order, piety, and safety in the church of the Lord Jesus" (*Bloudy Tenent*, 43). The radical purity of the church thus differs from the fundamental corruption of the world as a whole.

> The world lies in wickedness [declares Williams], is like a wilderness or a sea of wild beasts innumerable, fornicators, covetous, idolaters, &c. with whom God's people may lawfully converse and cohabit in cities, towns, &c., else must not live in the world but go out of it. In which world, as soon as ever the Lord Jesus had sown the good seed (the children of the Kingdom, true Christianity, or the true church), the enemy Satan presently in the night of security, ignorance, and error (whilst man slept), sowed also the tares which are antichristians or false Christians (*Bloudy Tenent*, 44).

The world of Williams is a wilderness; the church (insofar as Williams describes it at all) is a bright spot of purity. God so protects it that it is needless for men to offer it protection from the world around it: God is able to save His elect in any circumstance.

In Cotton's world, men are the potential means through which God acts. The pouring out of God's wrath, predicted in the Book of Revelation, is to come through the efforts of godly men, persecutors of corruption, even such men as the New England Congregationalists. He believes that it is lawful to punish those in a Christian commonwealth who attack religious truth because the state should protect the church from disturbances and because on fundamental points of religious doctrine and worship, the Bible is so clear that once one's error is explained to him by citing Scripture, he "cannot but be convinced of the dangerous error of his way" (*The Controversie* [1649], 7). After such an explanation, one cannot plead that he has a right to attack orthodoxy (Cotton's variety) for the sake of his conscience; indeed, to attack orthodoxy after admonition is to defy one's own conscience, and so one is liable to punishment.

There are three religious sins which Cotton would have the state punish: blasphemy, idolatry, and the seduction of others to one's errors. The first two are the ones concerning which Cotton says the Bible is perfectly clear. He would punish those who spread heresy because he put little faith in man's reason. He did not praise a fugitive and cloistered virtue: he saw the world as inevitably a dangerous place where risks are unavoidable. He sought to preserve the peace of a community which had unity, as his did. Though Cotton would vigorously reject modern pluralism, he was seeking a place in a pluralistic society for a unified community, founded on a voluntary covenant. He sought the establishment of the modern equivalent of ancient Israel, and in Massachusetts he wanted to protect the community as had the ancient injunction of Deuteronomy 13:9-10: "thou shalt surely kill him . . . because he hath sought to thrust thee away from the Lord thy God."

Cotton considers the magistrates of Massachusetts as the equivalent of the kings of Israel. Like the Old Testament prophets, Cotton teaches that, since God is just, He will visit an apostate land with punishment; to protect their people—

their bodies as well as their souls—the magistrates must not permit apostasy. The rulers are responsible to God for both body and soul. As a Puritan Cotton looked to the Bible for commandment and precedent, and for him the Old Testament provided magistrates with perfect models.

Williams too looked to the Bible, but unlike Cotton he saw a radical separation between the Old and the New Testaments. As Perry Miller has demonstrated, Williams was a typologist who believed that "the narrative of Israel . . . must be translated into the doctrines of Christianity. It is not really an account of kings and harlots but an allegory. When viewed in this light, the repressive and persecuting actions of Jewish sovereigns are not precedents for modern rulers, but typological pointers towards the methods by which, in the antitype, ministers should pronounce purely spiritual condemnations."[2]

That Williams supposed that he could persuade Cotton and the New Englanders to accept his allegorical interpretation of the Old Testament is difficult to imagine. Cotton and the other Congregationalists taught as fundamental doctrine that the same Covenant of Faith was offered in both Testaments; they looked to the Old Testament and to the example of Abraham as the authority for their idea of the church covenant.

Cotton's position on the relationship of church and state and his opposition to religious tolerance were closely identified with almost every aspect of his thought. He could scarcely have taken a different position in the debate with Williams. But Cotton would not have appeared quite so unmodern if Williams had not seen fit to blame Cotton for his being thrust out into the New England wilderness in midwinter. Williams went so far as to argue that if he had died "in that sorrowful winter's flight," Cotton would have been guilty of his death, for Cotton "without mercy and human compassion" caused him to "be exposed to winter miseries in a howling wilderness" (*Mr. Cottons Letter Lately Printed,* 1). This charge Cotton answered in the second part of *The Bloudy Tenent Washed,* but his book has not persuaded historians who should know that he was innocent of the charge. Cotton appears to have had truth on his side.

The truth is [declares Cotton] the sentence of his banishment out of the patent was pronounced against him in the Court before winter, and respite was given him to tarry certain weeks (six or more) to prepare for his journey. In the meantime, some of his friends went to the place appointed by himself beforehand to make provision of housing and other necessaries for him against his coming; otherwise he might have chosen to have gone southward to his acquaintance at Plymouth, or eastward to Pascatoque or Aganimticut. And then the wilderness had been as no wilderness (at least, no howling wilderness) where men sit down under warm and dry roofs, sheltered from the annoyance of frost and snow and other winter hardships.[3]

At the time of Williams' exile, the Bay Colony had not, as Edmund Morgan observes in *The Puritan Dilemma* (132), "been split apart or lured into such an irresponsible pursuit of individual holiness as Williams advocated. The great majority of the population, even the great majority of the Salem church, kept their eyes on the goal that Winthrop had set them. . . . a common goal which all must seek together. . . ." But by 1646 the goal was being neglected by many. Disillusionment over their great experiment, dissatisfaction with the Colony's government, attacks from the right and the left—all of these meant that the unity of the Colony was rapidly disappearing. This disappearance must have been evident to John Cotton, but in *The Bloudy Tenent Washed* he kept his eyes on his ideal, not on reality. Williams' desire to deny the state a holy purpose and to limit it to worldly, temporal functions struck at the very heart of Cotton's concept of a united purpose which binds all aspects of life to one another.

Williams won the debate; his *Bloudy Tenent* was burned in London by the public hangman, but the prestige of the New England Way had suffered from the exposé. Williams had the last word in the debate in *The Bloody Tenent Yet More Bloody, By Mr. Cottons endeavor to wash it White in the Blood of the Lambe* (1652). The trend of history too was on Williams' side, for when the Holy Commonwealth of Massachusetts Bay became a royal province in 1692, the process of secularization was completed. Today Williams is viewed as the prophet of the order which was to be.

CHAPTER 8

Moses and Aaron Kiss Each Other: The Political Writings

THOUGH JOHN WINTHROP is usually recognized as the chief spokesman for New England theocracy, it was John Cotton who was called on at a crucial time to describe and to defend the system of political government which had been established. Cotton did not himself have a hand in the ordering of the Massachusetts Bay political structure, just as he had not made the original ordering of the ecclesiastical structure. He was indeed influential in politics of both church and state, but perhaps these activities were less important than his services as a kind of forerunner of the modern public relations expert.

Because he was thoroughly sympathetic with the ideals of the Bay Colony, Cotton assumed an important role almost as soon as he arrived. In 1634 Winthrop consulted him when Roger Williams attacked the colonists' right to the lands which they were inhabiting. Cotton was called on again in 1636 to help decide how strict the discipline of the Colony should be. Indeed, Winthrop, who was governor during many of the early years, consulted Cotton frequently on many matters, as well he might, since he was a member of Cotton's church.

In addition, Cotton frequently found occasion in his sermons to deal with political matters. Thus he explained that the magistrates, who disagreed with the town representatives in a matter before the General Court, had a veto power and could prevent the adoption of a measure though they were outvoted.

Cotton was not alone in his close relationship as minister to the political powers. Norton, Cotton's biographer, tells us that

It was an usual thing . . . for the magistrates to consult with the ministers in hard cases, especially in matters of the Lord; yet so as, notwithstanding occasional conjunction, religious care was had of avoiding confusion of counsels. Moses and Aaron rejoiced and kissed one another in the Mount of God. . . . how useful he [Cotton] was to England, to magistrates, to ministers, to people, in public and in private, by preaching, counsel, and resolving difficult questions, all know that knew him.[1]

Perry Miller puts Cotton's role more simply; he was "the mouthpiece of the ruling oligarchy."[2]

I *Answer to Lord Say*

The letter to Lord Say and Seal—discussed in the chapter on Congregationalism because of the treatment in the letter of the political covenant—was written in answer to a letter which Lord Say, Lord Brooke, and "other persons of quality" had written in 1636 to Henry Vane. Cotton also wrote answers to ten demands which the lords had sent to Vane. Cotton had first sought out "such leading men amongst us as I thought meet to consult withal,"[3] but the letter itself was his responsibility.

The lords had proposed that they, along with others of their social rank, should constitute the equivalent of the House of Lords in the new colony, with the lords having veto power. These gentlemen would become the hereditary aristocracy of the colony. The other class to have political power, the freeholders, was to be limited to large landowners who "have contributed some fit proportion to the public charge of the country either by their disbursements or labors" (Hutchinson, I, 412).

The Americans would have none of it, though they could see that their present system of political power could in part be interpreted as consistent with what the lords wanted. But Cotton's reply is thoroughly diplomatic:

As for accepting them ["these noble personages and worthy gentlemen"] and their heirs into the number of gentlemen of the country, the custom of this country is, and readily would be, to receive and acknowledge not only all such eminent persons as themselves and the gentlemen they speak of, but others of meaner estate, so be it of some eminency, to be for them and their heirs gentlemen of the country. Only thus standeth our case. Though we receive them with honor and allow them pre-eminence and accommodations according to their condition, yet we do not, ordinarily, call them forth to the power of election or administration of magistracy, until they be received as members into some of our churches, a privilege which we doubt not religious gentlemen will willingly desire (as David did in Psalm xxvii.4) and Christian churches will as readily impart to such desirable persons. Hereditary honors both nature and Scripture doth acknowledge (Ecclesiastes xix.17), but hereditary authority and power standeth only by the civil laws of some common-wealths, and yet, even amongst them, the authority and power of the father is nowhere communicated, together with his honors, unto all his posterity. Where God blesseth any branch of any noble or generous family, with a spirit and gifts fit for government, it would be a taking of God's name in vain to put such a talent under a bushel, and a sin against the honor of magistracy to neglect such in our public elections. But if God should not delight to furnish some of their posterity with gifts fit for magistracy, we should expose them rather to reproach and prejudice, and the commonwealth with them, than exalt them to honor, if we should call them forth, when God doth not, to public authority (412).

These were brave words in 1636. They suggest a dedication to an ideal at a time when the Colony was in real need of financial assistance. The understanding which Cotton shows of the nature of the venture was surely one of the reasons for his power and influence.

II An Abstract of the Laws

On May 6, 1635, according to John Winthrop, "The deputies having conceived great danger to our state in regard that our magistrates, for want of positive laws in many cases, might proceed according to their discretions, it was agreed that some men should be appointed to frame a body of grounds of law, in resemblance to a Magna Carta, which, being allowed by some of the ministers and the General Court, should be received for fundamental laws."[4] Those appointed to prepare the Massachusetts Magna Carta were the governor, John Haynes; two former governors, John Winthrop and Thomas Dudley; and a future governor, Richard Bellingham. Nothing was accomplished. A year later another committee was appointed, this time with

Governor Henry Vane, Winthrop, Dudley, Haynes, and three ministers, Thomas Shepard, Hugh Peter, and John Cotton.

As a member of this committee Cotton presented to the General Court in October, 1636, what Winthrop called "a model of Moses his judicials, compiled in an exact method" (*Journal*, I, 196). The code circulated for five years but finally was not adopted because it was not what was needed: a bill of rights to set limits to the power of the magistrates. Instead what Cotton prepared was in the main a compilation of the laws already established, supplemented by many proposals consistent with these laws. The work was published twice, in 1641 and in 1655, first as *An Abstract, or The Lawes of New England as they are now established* and later as *An Abstract of Laws and Government*. Though not adopted, it had considerable influence, as we shall see.

Sometime between his presentation of the laws and the Court's rejection of them, Cotton defended his proposal; and a manuscript copy in Cotton's hand of his defense is extant. Entitled "How Far Moses Judicialls Bind Massachusetts," it was published as part of Worthington C. Ford's "Cotton's 'Moses his Judicials.' "[5] In it Cotton distinguishes two types of Old Testament law, temporary and perpetual. The latter he considers binding on Massachusetts, and he offers nine reasons. Some of them are: "because God, who was then bound up in covenant with them [the Hebrews] to be their God, hath put us in their stead and is become our God as well as theirs, and hence we are as much bound to their laws as well as themselves"; "if God hath given us no other for the governing of the commonwealth, then we either may be lawless and have what laws we please or else be bound to these, but God hath given us no other nor are we lawless, for we are under the Law to God and to Christ"; adoption of God's laws "will be our wisdom in the sight of the nations (Deuteronomy iv.6) so as they shall say, this is a wise people"; "if the Jews be now still under the bond of them and so to observe them when they are an established commonwealth, then we are bound to observe them . . . because there is no other revelation that they shall be other laws" (281). Added later is a thoroughly Puritan reason for following biblical law: "The more any law smells of man, the more unprofitable" (284).

Cotton describes in an interesting passage the relationship of the Old Testament to Christianity. As reconstructed, it reads:

> If it was a part of the misery of [the] Gentiles to be aliens from the commonwealth of Israel (Ephesians ii.12), then 'tis a part of the hap[piness] of Christian nations that they are subject to the laws of that commonwealth of Israel; and [to be] strangers from the commonwealth of Israel is not [to be a] church because that is [to be] strangers from the promise, [that is,] from [the] covenant of [the] church and so from [the] civil covenant. Christ is king of church and commonwealth. So far as it [the church] varies from the commonwealth of Israel, so [far is Christ] from [being] king of the church. So far [as the commonwealth varies] from the laws of [the] church, [so far is Christ from being] king of [the] commonwealth. Christ is head of all principalities and powers for the church, and He will subordinate all kingdoms one day to the church (284).

Here is the basis for the organicism of the Colony.

Cotton's *Abstract* is divided into ten chapters. The first, concerning the magistrates, as a whole follows Massachusetts policy, but it provides lifetime tenure for the assistants "because these great affairs of the state cannot be attended nor administered if they be after changed" (1641 ed., p. 2). To support his position, Cotton cites I Kings 12:6: "And King Rehoboam consulted with the old men, that stood before Solomon his father while he yet lived, and said, How do ye advise that I may answer this people?" Here Cotton remained consistent with what he had preached at the General Court in 1634, that "a magistrate ought not to be turned into the condition of a private man without just cause, and to be publicly convict, no more than the magistrates may not turn a private man out of his freehold, etc., without like public trial, etc." (*Journal*, I, 124-25). The Court had answered Cotton by choosing several new magistrates and by turning out the old ones.

Cotton says surprisingly little in *The Abstract* about the relationship of the magistrates to the church, merely that the governor has power "to preserve religion." But this power is great indeed, as later chapters make clear. More is said about the kind of person to be chosen magistrate: a free burgess (Cotton's equivalent of freeman) "out of the ablest men and most approved amongst them," and "out of the rank of noblemen or gentlemen among them, the best that God shall send into the country, if they be qualified with gifts fit for government, either eminent above others, or not inferior to others" (1). It is not surprising that Cotton should make this recommendation, for in 1634 he had lectured the inhabitants of Boston for their failure to elect Winthrop "and other of the chief men" to a committee on land distribution (Winthrop, *Journal*, I, 143-44).

Chapter II, "Of the Free Burgesses and Free Inhabitants," defines the power of the burgesses as electors and the power of the General Court elected by the burgesses. Cotton explains in it more of his view of the relation of church and state. The General Court is "to assist the governors and counselors in the maintenance of the purity and unity of religion, and accordingly to set forward and uphold all such good causes as shall be thought fit for that end by the advice with consent of the churches, and to repress the contrary" (3-4).

Although it is often maintained that Cotton's code is purely Old Testament legalism, he does not attempt to support any of the articles of this chapter by reference to Scripture. The same can be said for Chapter III, most of Chapter IV, and most of Chapter IX. English common law and the established practices of the Colony are nearly as important as the Bible as foundations for *The Abstract*.

Chapter III, "Of the Protection and Provision of the Country," deals with taxes, the military, and fishing. In it Cotton proposes a law to promote commercial fishing by providing men "to plant and to reap" for the fishermen, mariners, and shipbuilders for the next seven years (4). Though nothing so generous appears to have been done, a law was passed in 1639 which remitted the taxes for seven years on all fishing supplies and materials.

Religion is a concern even in Chapter IV, "Of the Right of Inheritance." Here we also find that no one is permitted to dwell more than a mile from a church meeting house, for "all civil affairs are to be administered and ordered so as may best conduce to the upholding and setting forward of the worship of God in church fellowship" (6). In dividing the lands of a town, Cotton would have two considerations determine the amount of land to be awarded: the size of the family (plus the number of animals owned) and the character of the prospective landowner. "Eminent respect in this case may be given to men of eminent quality and descent in assigning unto them more large and honorable accommodations in regard of their great disbursements to public charges" (6). This proposal was carried out when lands owned by Boston at Muddy River were divided. Cotton was given 250 acres, while the less prosperous citizens were granted only eight acres.

Much of this chapter is concerned with arrangements to prevent the loss of taxes should land be sold to someone other than an inhabitant of the town wherein the land lies. But one provision in this chapter is curious and difficult to explain. Instead of following English common law which permitted a man to will his estate as he saw fit, Cotton provides that the eldest son is to have a double portion. He cites in support Deuteronomy 21:17. Cotton's plan of inheritance was in fact adopted by the General Court.[6]

Chapter V, "Of Commerce," again may indicate Cotton's influence on Massachusetts policies, or it may indicate merely that Cotton accepted what appeared to be the only solution to a difficult situation. From its early years Massachusetts had fixed prices and profits, but variation in supply and demand made regulation difficult. Cotton urged the establishment of township committees to handle the problem, a solution which in time was partially adopted by the General Court, who assigned wage-level problems to the towns.[7] In 1639, because Robert Keayne was found guilty of making too large a profit on commodities, Cotton preached from the pulpit on false and sound principles of buying and selling. A summary of Cotton's views appears in Winthrop's *Journal* (I, 317-18). The chapter in *The Abstract* discusses other matters of business ethics, such as borrowing; but it does not offer a really adequate program for a business community.

The chapter "Of Trespasses" is fuller than might be expected, presumably because Cotton found many Hebrew laws on the subject in Exodus and Leviticus. Similarly full is the list of crimes deserving capital punishment. Nineteen crimes are cited in Chapter VII, including sixteen supported by biblical citations: blasphemy; idolatry; witchcraft; consulting with witches; heresy with attempt to seduce others; worshipping God in a molten or graven image; Sabbath breaking; rebellion, sedition, and insurrection; rebelliousness on the part of children; murder; adultery; incest; sodomy and buggery; intercourse with a woman during her monthly period; "whoredom of a maiden in her father's house"; man stealing; and bearing false witness. Only three non-biblical crimes are to be punished by death: willful perjury, treason, and reviling the governor or his counselors.

The list sounds impressively severe. In fact, English law of the time was much more severe. It provided death for stealing more than a shilling, for housebreaking, and for many other crimes. Most of the crimes on Cotton's list were cause for capital punishment in England. Rebellious children in England were not subject to the death sentence, as they were in Massachusetts; and English adulterers were liable only to heavy fines. But unnatural sex acts, heresy, witchcraft, all were capital offenses.[8] The only peculiarly Puritan crime here is Sabbath breaking, and the Puritans of England shared Cotton's concern to keep the day holy. *The Lawes and Liberties of Massachusetts* (6) followed Cotton in prescribing death for adultery and for intercourse with a woman espoused but not yet married.

Lesser crimes were to be punished less severely than in England, according to Chapter VIII. Cotton names only seven lesser crimes: profanity, drunkenness, rape, fornication, maiming or wounding, theft, and slander. All of these were also punishable by English law. Cotton proposes as punishments—depending on the crime—fines, whipping, branding, or boring through the tongue. A rapist, for example, is to be punished with "fine or penalty to the father of the maid. 2. With marriage of the maid defiled, if she and her father consent. 3. With corporal punishment of stripes for his wrong, as a real slander" (12).

Chapter IX, concerning trials and execution of sentences, reveals clearly that Cotton is familiar with and favorably disposed toward English common law. He provides for an impartial jury in criminal and civil cases, and he forbids the imprisonment of any man unless he has been convicted or is suspected of having committed a crime named specifically in the code.

The final chapter, "Of Causes Criminal Between Our People and Foreign Nations," is perhaps the most interesting and probably the most original. Cotton briefly explains the justification for war: when the people of another nation do "any important wrong to any of ours" and "right and justice be denied and it will not stand with the honor of God and safety of our nation that the wrong be passed over, then war is to be undertaken and denounced" (14). For such a war, men are to be spared from the army if they are betrothed but not married, or recently married, or "have newly built or planted and not received the fruits of their labors," or if they are "fainthearted men."

Cotton devotes three sections to the spoils of war. He is particularly interested in sparing fruit trees and women, "especially such as have not lain by men." He gives the church its share of the spoils, a larger one if all of the soldiers survive and return.

The Abstract, or *Moses His Judicials*, is an interesting and important work, and not merely a curiosity. Miss Calder argues that it "deserves recognition as the earliest compilation of New England legislation" (94). She notes that Cotton's code was adopted in 1639 as a permanent constitution for the New Haven Colony, and that it was also used by the company which settled at Southampton, Long Island, in 1640. A more recent commentator, George L. Haskins, finds it remarkable that Cotton, "who had no legal training and who was not an officer of the colony, should have had as complete a grasp as he did of the fundamentals of its government, of the laws already in existence, and of the need in certain directions for guarantees of due process and civil rights."[9]

III A Discourse about Civil Government

Closely related to *The Abstract* is *A Discourse about Civil Government in a New Plantation Whose Design is Religion* (Cambridge, Mass., 1663).[10] The *Discourse* is a letter apparently to the Reverend John Davenport, a founder of the New Haven Colony and a house guest of Cotton's in 1637. Davenport seems to have been sympathetic to Cotton's legal code in every respect but one. He was not sure that Cotton (and Massachusetts) was right to restrict to church members the right to vote and to hold office. Cotton's letter of explanation and defense is valuable for the light it sheds on his view of the relationship of church and state. It is an important document, one strangely overlooked by most scholars.

Cotton distinguishes the role and function of church and state as follows: "Man by nature being a reasonable and sociable creature, capable of civil order, is or may be the subject of civil power and state, but man by grace called out of the world to fellowship with Jesus Christ and with His people is the only subject of church power" (6). Cotton defines the state as "an human order appointed by God to men for civil fellowship of human things" (6). Church and state are thus parallel institutions but with separate purposes.

The best form of government for a Christian commonwealth is, according to Cotton, a "theocraty," the form of government which exists when "all the free burgesses be such as are in fellowship of the church or churches which are or may be gathered according to Christ," and when "those free burgesses have the only power of choosing from among themselves civil magistrates" (14).

If the magistrates are all church members, then they will rule by God's laws. They have power over their old failings and are endowed with the power of the Holy Spirit. If all magistrates are church members, they can work together in peace and harmony and also consult with the ministers of God "in all hard cases and in matters of religion" (15). A state like this is the form of government prescribed by the Old Testament example of Israel, Cotton points out, and also the type of government which gives Christ what Saint Paul says is due to Him.

Though Christ is over both church and state, there is no confusion of the two in Cotton's plan. The corruption of the Papacy developed, he says, when the civil power delegated authority to ecclesiastical officers. But as members of the church, civil officers are spiritually subject to ecclesiastical officers. One provides outward honor, justice, and civil peace; the other, the means of grace, pardon of sin, and peace with God.

Cotton's description of the relationship of church and state indicates his great concern with the problem. It should be emphasized that he was addressing men who were planning a colony "whose design is religion." Unlike some critics of the early American Puritans, we would do well to note what their motives were before we judge them to have been hypocrites.

Cotton's political writings reveal more clearly than those of any other New England writer the organic nature of the Massachusetts Bay Colony in its early years. Church and state, laws and economic forces, all were interrelated. To call Cotton the high priest of Puritan theocracy is perhaps a judgment and not a description; Cotton would have preferred to think of himself as one who played the roles of both Moses and Aaron.

Tamer of Impious Sentiments:
The Poems

NEW ENGLAND PURITANS wrote and read a good deal
more poetry than used to be supposed, but little of the
poetry produced, except for Edward Taylor's, has much literary
value. Like Taylor, most of the lesser Puritan poets tried to fuse
wit and sentiment. For example, John Fiske, whose poetry was
rediscovered recently by Harold Jantz, wrote an elegy on the
death of John Cotton in the form of variations on an anagram
of the dead preacher's name: "O, Honie Knott." Though the poem
seems more ingenious than powerful, Fiske's "But now, oh and
alas to thee to call/In vain 'tis" presumably was meant to sound
quite heartfelt.[1]

Kenneth Murdock has suggested that the inadequacies of
American Puritan poetry can be explained partly by a consideration of the poet's audience. A poet wrote "to be of service
to the rank and file of his readers."[2] In a closed community such
as the Massachusetts Bay Colony tended to be, the preacher
frequently felt obliged to speak words of consolation to his flock
or to that of a dead colleague. Thus Fiske, pastor at Salem,
wrote consolatory verses on the deaths of the Reverends Nathaniel
Rogers, Thomas Hooker, Samuel Sharpe (ruling elder of his own
church), and John Wilson.

Wilson, Cotton's colleague in the ministry of the church at
Boston, was a poet of some note in his lifetime, more because he
was a pious preacher than because he was accomplished in the
art of poetry. John Cotton too was interested in poetry, as his
book *Singing of Psalms* shows. He may have made some of the
translations of the Psalms as they appear in the Bay Psalm Book.

Cotton wrote five extant poems, according to Harold Jantz in *The First Century of New England Verse* (193), and Donald Come has located a fragment of another, to which he refers in his unpublished Princeton dissertation on Cotton.[3]

The fragment, probably written in the 1610's, is interesting for its content rather than for its art. Apparently written before Cotton became a non-conformist, it seems to identify him as a moral Puritan, not an opponent of ceremonies, if indeed he considered himself a Puritan at all. The verse is as follows:

> Of Puritans two sorts I find,
> The moral and the ceremonial kind:
> The ceremonial, God's great name to hallow,
> Will strain at motes, as well as beams not swallow.
> His tender conscience makes his fleshly heart
> At smallest pricks and scruples back to start.

The earliest of the five complete poems is a consolatory verse written after he had decided to give up Lincolnshire for Massachusetts Bay. Poetry was for Cotton, as for other Puritans, a means of taming one's emotions by forcing them into the pattern demanded by art. The fact that he needed this kind of discipline at the time of his self-exile suggests that it was a wrenching experience for him. The poem is not so bad as to suggest that this kind of writing was utterly unfamiliar to Cotton. The third and fourth of the eight stanzas read:

> When I think of the sweet and gracious company
> That at BOSTON once I had,
> And of the long peace of a fruitful ministry,
> For twenty years enjoy'd:
>
> The joy that I found in all that happiness
> Doth still so much refresh me
> That the grief to be cast out into a wilderness
> Doth not so much distress me.

The second, also consolatory, was written for those who bewailed the loss of Thomas Hooker in 1647. Prefixed to Hooker's *Survey of the Summe of Church–Discipline*, the poem "On my Reverend and dear Brother Mr. Thomas Hooker" is in many ways Cotton's best. Following the fashion of the day, it combines wit with piety. The thesis of the poem is that in Hooker was found the equivalent of what Saint Augustine had wished to see: "Rome in her flower" (Hooker offered more, for the beauty of Zion shone in his rule and doctrine); "Christ Jesus in the flesh" (Hooker's preaching provided what was better, the Spirit of Christ); and "Paul i' the pulpit" (Hooker inherited a double portion of Paul's spirit). The poem ends with this coda:

> Now, blessed Hooker, thou art set on high,
> Above the thankless world and cloudy sky:
> Do thou of all thy labor reap the crown,
> Whilst we here reap the seed which thou hast sown.

The third poem Cotton Mather located on a spare leaf of John Cotton's almanac. In three parts, the poem—in Mather's words—"most exemplarily expressed what was required" when Rowland and Sarah, Cotton's youngest son and eldest daughter, died of smallpox during the fall of 1649. The occasion was apparently too much for the father, for the poem is probably Cotton's weakest. It reads, in part:

> On th' twentieth of th' eleventh died she,
> And on the twenty-ninth day died he.
> Both in their lives were lovely and united,
> And in their deaths they were not much divided.

The fact that Cotton felt obliged to be witty is surely one reason for the failure of the poem.

More successful because the wit seems more natural is the poem on Samuel Stone, Hooker's colleague in the ministry of the Hartford church. The poem, a eulogy written for Stone when he was still alive to enjoy it, plays with the minister's name by identifying him with stones having religious significance. Stone is "for solid firmness fit to rear/A part in Zion's wall"; he is—most playfully—"Like Samuel's stone, erst Ebenezer hight,/To tell the Lord hath help'd us with His might."

Finally, Cotton wrote a five-stanza autobiography in verse entitled "A Thankful Acknowledgment of God's Providence." It suggests that the disappointments which marked his last years did not altogether sour him.

In mother's womb Thy fingers did me make,
  And from the womb Thou didst me safely take:
From breast Thou hast me nurs'd my life throughout,
  That I may say I never wanted ought.

In all my meals my table Thou hast spread,
  In all my lodgings Thou hast made my bed:
Thou hast me clad with changes of array,
  And chang'd my house for better far away.

In youthful wanderings Thou didst stay my slide,
  In all my journeys Thou hast been my guide:
Thou hast me sav'd from many an unknown danger,
  And show'd me favor, even where I was a stranger.

In both my callings Thou hast heard my voice,
  In both my matches Thou hast made my choice:
Thou gav'st me sons and daughters, them to peer,
  And giv'st me hope thou'lt learn them Thee to fear.

Oft have I seen Thee look with mercy's face,
  And through Thy Christ have felt Thy saving grace,
This is the Heav'n on earth, if any be:
  For this, and all, my soul doth worship Thee.

Cotton's poetry is the least of his accomplishments, but for this last poem we can be grateful, for it suggests that the gentleness and the serenity which so often come through in his sermons were based on an experiential religion, about which Cotton has almost nothing to say, at least directly, in his other writings.

CHAPTER *10*

John Cotton's Significance and Contribution to American Literature

THE PECULIAR QUALITY of early American Puritan culture—what we have called its organicism—is to a considerable extent the work of John Cotton, whose activities
touched many sides of this culture. The sense of mission which he
felt throughout his American career—and during a good part
of his years in England—lies behind this organicism too. From
the days of his ministry in Lincolnshire, Cotton's thinking was
dominated by his dream of purity, of the covenanted community.
But always mixed with this idealism was a tendency to be
cautious, to be conservative. This quality is indicated by Cotton's
waiting until three years after the Massachusetts Bay Colony
had been established before making his move to join it. Perhaps
it is not too much to say that this mixture of conservatism and
idealism is what characterized New England culture as late as
the time of Emerson, though in the eighteenth century conservatism seemed for a time triumphant.

Cotton alone was not, of course, responsible. His traits are
found in John Winthrop and in such diverse personalities as
Richard Mather and Nathaniel Ward. But Cotton had other
qualities that are also "typically New England." He was more
concerned with the practical than the theoretical, with the
working of church government than the details of theology. He
was inspired by other men's ideas—John Calvin's and William
Ames's and Richard Sibbes's. He was a scholar but not an
original thinker. He had a strong sense of the moment, what
Larzer Ziff calls "the eschatological tone," "a sense of the
American experience as one of changes hastening along to one

millennium or another."[1] This blend of qualities does not make Cotton an attractive figure—we prefer the originality and liberalism of a Roger Williams to Cotton's caution. But, as Daniel Boorstin observes, if the Puritans had had other qualities, "they might have merited praise as precursors of modern liberalism, but they might never have helped found a nation."[2]

No single work of Cotton's demonstrates all these qualities, and no one work stands out as his masterpiece. Some of Cotton's best writings can of course be identified. The letter to Lord Say and Seal, the first three sermons in *Gods Mercie Mixed with his Iustice,* early pages from *The Powrring out of the Seven Vials, Milk for Babes,* passages in *The Way Cleared,* and parts of *The Bloudy Tenent Washed*—these are Cotton's best. All are distinguished by their intellectuality, their clarity, and their authority. But there is a bloodlessness, a lack of warmth that arouses no enthusiasm, only respect. Beside the extravagances of his grandson Cotton Mather, John Cotton is commendably classical in his restraint; yet one misses thunder and fire such as one gets from Thomas Hooker.

But one comes back to an appreciation of Cotton's sense of mission, to the understanding which his works give of the religious nature of the undertaking in Massachusetts. Beside the heroic efforts of the Plymouth Pilgrims, the settlers of Massachusetts Bay may appear to have been dominated by economic motives. Cotton's works reveal that economic factors were indeed recognized as having importance in the venture, but it was part of the breadth of the Puritan design that church and state, law and government, manners and morals, business and labor, all should find a place in the New England Way.

Kenneth Murdock writes with respect of the earlier New England Puritans as non-conformists (in the popular sense of the word), and he quotes with approval Emerson's opinion that the essence of Boston is its principle of rebellion, started before "pioneer Puritanism hardened down into an organized and intolerant ecclesiastical and creedal system."[3] John Cotton was a pioneer Puritan Bostonian, but even in his less than twenty years in the American wilderness we can detect the hardening of his values into a system. It was in part a consequence of his unpleasant experiences with the Hutchinsonians which created this cautious and conservative spirit, and in part his disappoint-

ment over the failure to have Congregationalism adopted by
England. But Cotton appears always to have been on the side
of stability and authority, though he taught that authority itself
must be limited. (It is characteristic of Cotton to insist that
magistrates are to have extensive powers but still *limited* powers:
they should be given "as much power as God in His Word gives
to men," not more (*An Exposition upon The Thirteenth Chapter
of the Revelation* [1655], 72).

Most of all, there was the influence of Congregationalism on
Cotton. The New England Way involved the perpetual balancing
off of the democratic tendencies and the autocratic ones, the
Separatist tendency to assume a superior purity and the natural
tendency to assume that whatever is being done is right. Shut
off from the larger world of Europe, Cotton did well to prevent
American values from becoming identified with extremism and
with fanaticism, as they did with some of his successors.

Although influences are hard to pin down, John Cotton as
the most representative and probably the most popular writer
of his generation in America appears to have been an important
influence on American literature. The simplicity of Franklin and
Edwards appears to have been the consequence of the Puritan
ideal of plainness. In England the change from the baroque
ornateness of Sir Thomas Browne to the simple clarity of John
Dryden resulted in part from the influence of Puritan plain style.[4]

Cotton is a difficult writer to resurrect. He is minor indeed,
but for Americans not to be ignored. Cotton's devotion to
scholarship, his willingness to take a risk, his idealism and his
conservatism—these are in the great American tradition. His
mildness makes his prose less lively than Thomas Hooker's and
Thomas Shepard's, but the greater variety of his works gives
them real importance. He who would understand the rationale
of the Massachusetts Bay Colony ignores at his peril the writings
of John Cotton.

Notes and References

Chapter One

1. Bush, *English Literature in the Earlier Seventeenth Century* (Oxford, 1945), p. 296.
2. On the transformation of Puritanism in the 1640's, see Charles George's excellent study, "A Social Interpretation of English Puritanism," *Journal of Modern History,* XXV (1953), 327-42.
3. Ziff, *The Career of John Cotton* (Princeton, 1962), pp. viii, 159.
4. Miller, "The Cambridge Platform in 1648," in H. W. Foote, ed., *The Cambridge Platform of 1648* (Boston, 1949), p. 70.
5. Norton, *Memoir of John Cotton* (Boston, 1834), p. 25.

Chapter Two

1. Cotton is inconsistent here with his letter of resignation to Bishop John Williams. There he cites his "bodily health" and "the peace of the Church" as his reasons for leaving, though he does note that he had not discerned that he had "Christian liberty to practice some commands of authority in some circumstances" (*Chronicles of the First Planters,* ed. Alexander Young, Boston, 1846, pp. 434-36).

Chapter Three

1. Haller, *The Rise of Puritanism* (New York, 1938), p. 15.
2. Sibbes, *Works* (Edinburgh, 1862-1864), I, 53.
3. Smith, *Works* (Edinburgh, 1866-1867), I, 304-5.
4. Adams, *Works,* (London, 1629), p. 433.
5. Norton, *Memoir of John Cotton* (Boston, 1834), pp. 38-39.
6. See my study, "John Udall and the Puritan Sermon," *Quarterly Journal of Speech,* XLIV (1958), 282-84.
7. Shepard, *The Sincere Convert* (London, 1672), p. 62; the work was first published in 1640.
8. Baynes, *A Counterbane* (London, 1618), p. 19.
9. Max Weber, *The Protestant Ethic and the Spirit of Capitalism* (London, 1930), p. 232.
10. Heppe, *Reformed Dogmatics* (London, 1950), p. 521.

11. Calvin, *The Deity of Christ and Other Sermons,* trans. Leroy Nixon (Grand Rapids, 1950), pp. 151-52.

Chapter Four

1. Winthrop, "A Model of Christian Charity," in Perry Miller and Thomas H. Johnson, eds., *The Puritans* (New York, 1938), pp. 197, 199.

2. The later attitude is explored in Perry Miller, *The New England Mind: From Colony to Province* (Cambridge, Mass., 1953).

3. See Larzer Ziff, *The Career of John Cotton* (Princeton, 1962), pp. 76-90.

4. Stearns, *The Strenuous Puritan: Hugh Peter, 1598-1660* (Urbana, Ill., 1954), p. 174.

5. Haller, *Liberty and Reformation in the Puritan Revolution* (New York, 1955), p. 155.

6. Quoted by Williston Walker, *A History of the Congregational Churches in the United States* (New York, 1916), p. 108.

7. Hutchinson, *History of Massachusetts Bay* (Cambridge, Mass., 1936), I, 415.

8. Quoted in Perry Miller, *Orthodoxy in Massachusetts* (Cambridge, Mass., 1933), p. 158.

9. See Ziff, "The Social Bond of Church Covenant," *American Quarterly,* X (1958), 454-62.

10. Quoted in Miller, *From Colony to Province,* p. 256.

11. Edwards, *Antapologia* (London, 1644), pp. 31-32, 40.

12. Williston Walker, ed., *The Creeds and Platforms of Congregationalism* (Boston, 1960), pp. 169-70.

13. Quoted by Ziff, "The Social Bond," p. 461.

Chapter Five

1. On May 16, 1626, he had, however, written Archbishop Ussher that "Christ Himself preached repentance, before faith in the promises. Neither do I remember in the Gospel any promise of grace pardoning sin, nor any commandment to believe sin pardoned, but to the broken, the bruised, the weary, the thirsty, or the like. Faith in the promises, before the heart be changed from stoniness to brokenness, I fear is not better than the temporary faith which is found in the stony soil." James Ussher, *Works,* ed. Charles R. Elrington (Dublin, 1864), XV, 331.

2. Ziff, *The Career of John Cotton* (Princeton, 1962), p. 113.

3. On his distinction, see Ernest Troeltsch, *The Social Teachings of the Christian Churches* (London, 1949), II, 590.

4. Foster, *A Genetic History of the New England Theology* (Chicago, 1907), p. 30, note.

5. Morgan, *The Puritan Family* (Boston, 1944).

6. Sasek, *The Literary Temper of the English Puritans* (Baton Rouge, 1961), p. 41.

Chapter Six

1. William Cunningham, *The Reformers and the Theology of the Reformation* (Edinburgh, 1866), p. 412.

2. Fuller, *Church History of Britain* (Oxford, 1845), V, 227.

3. See Battis, *Saints and Sectaries* (Chapel Hill, 1962), and Morgan, "The Case Against Anne Hutchinson," *New England Quarterly*, X (1937), 635-48. The background information in this chapter is based in the main on Battis and to a lesser extent on Charles Francis Adams, *Three Episodes of Massachusetts History*, 2 vols. (Boston, 1892).

4. Winthrop, "A Model," in Perry Miller and Thomas H. Johnson, eds., *The Puritans* (New York, 1938), p. 198.

5. Hooker, *The Soules Implantation* (London, 1637), p. 130.

6. Shepard, *The Saints Jewel* (London, 1672), pp. 188-90.

7. Shepard, *The Sincere Convert* (London, 1672), p. 33.

8. Hooker, *A Comment Upon Christ's last Prayer* (London, 1656), p. 7.

9. Hooker, *Spiritual Munition* (London, 1638), p. 25.

10. Hooker, *A Survey of the Summe of Church-Discipline* (London, 1648), Pt. 2, p. 19.

11. Perry Miller, *The New England Mind: From Colony to Province* (Cambridge, Mass., 1953), p. 62.

12. Battis, *Saints and Sectaries*, p. 172.

13. Cotton Papers, Boston Public Library, Pt. II, no. 12.

14. Parkes, "Morals and Law Enforcement in Colonial New England," *New England Quarterly*, V (1932), 431-52.

15. See Ames, *The Marrow of Sacred Divinity* (London, 1638 [?]), p. 209.

16. *The Lawes and Liberties of Massachusetts* (Cambridge, 1929), p. 11.

Chapter Seven

1. This account of Williams' career is based on Ola E. Winslow, *Master Roger Williams* (New York, 1957) and Edmund S. Morgan, *The Puritan Dilemma: The Story of John Winthrop* (Boston, 1958).

2. Miller, *Roger Williams* (New York, 1962), pp. 33-34.

3. Cotton, pp. 7-8. A defense of the banishment of Roger Williams is Henry M. Dexter's *As to Roger Williams* (Boston, 1876).

Chapter Eight

1. Norton, *Memoir of John Cotton* (Boston, 1834), p. 47.

2. Miller, "Thomas Hooker and the Democracy of Early Connecticut," *New England Quarterly*, IV (1931), 676.

3. Thomas Hutchinson, *The History of Massachusetts Bay* (Cambridge, Mass., 1936), I, 417.

4. Winthrop, *Journal* (New York, 1908), I, 151. The following account of *An Abstract of the Laws of New England* is much indebted to Isabel Calder, "John Cotton's 'Moses His Judicials,'" *Pubs. Col. Soc. Mass.*, XXVIII (1930-33), 86-94.

5. Ford, *Proc. Mass. Hist. Soc.*, 2nd Ser., XVI (1903), 274-84.

6. See *The Lawes and Liberties of Massachusetts* (Cambridge, Mass., 1929), pp. 53-54.

7. See Bernard Bailyn, *The New England Merchants in the Seventeenth Century* (Cambridge, Mass., 1955), p. 33.

8. See James F. Stephen, *A History of the Criminal Law of England*, 3 vols. (London, 1883).

9. Haskins, *Law and Authority in Early Massachusetts* (New York, 1960), p. 126.

10. For Cotton's authorship, see Isabel M. Calder, "The Authorship of *A Discourse About Civil Government*," *American Historical Review*, XXXVII (1932), 267-69. See also Miss Calder's "John Cotton and the New Haven Colony," *New England Quarterly*, III (1930), 82-94.

Chapter Nine

1. Harold Jantz, *The First Century of New England Verse* (New York, 1962), pp. 118-19.

2. Murdock, *Literature & Theology in Colonial New England* (New York, 1963), p. 143.

3. See the Bibliography for the sources of the texts of Cotton's poems.

Chapter Ten

1. Ziff, *The Career of John Cotton* (Princeton, 1962), pp. 160-61.

2. Boorstin, *The Americans: The Colonial Experience* (New York, 1958), p. 9.

3. Murdock, *Literature & Theology in Colonial New England* (New York, 1963), p. 189.

4. See Harold Fisch, "The Puritans and the Reform of Prose Style," *ELH*, XIX (1952), 229-48.

Selected Bibliography

PRIMARY SOURCES

The works of John Cotton are listed below in something like their order of composition, which is often difficult to determine. Dates of publication follow. It has not seemed useful to cite publishers for works published before 1800.

A. Works

1618   *A Treatise of Mr. Cottons, Clearing certaine Doubts concerning Predestination. Together with an Examination Thereof: written by William Twisse, D. D.* London, 1646.

1618   *Some Treasure Fetched out of Rubbish.* London, 1660.

1620- *A Practical Commentary . . . upon The First Epistle Generall*
1630   *of John.* London, 1656, 1658.

1622- *Gods Mercie Mixed with his Iustice.* London, 1641; Gaines-
1632   ville, Florida: Scholars' Facsimiles & Reprints, 1958. Reprinted as *The Saints Support & Comfort.* London, 1658.

1624- *The way of Life.* London, 1641.
1632

1624- *A Brief Exposition Of the Whole Book of Canticles, or, Song*
1632   *of Solomon.* London, 1642, 1648; Edinburgh: John Nichol, 1868.

1624- *Christ The Fountaine of Life.* London, 1651 (twice).
1632

1628   Prefatory epistle in Arthur Hildersam, *Lectures upon the Fourth of John.* London, 1629.

1630   *Gods Promise to his Plantation.* London, 1630, 1634, 1689; Boston: Old South Leaflets [1894].

1634   *A Treatise I. Of Faith. II. Twelve Fundamental Articles of Christian Religion. III. A Doctrinal Conclusion. IV. Questions and answers upon Church-Government.* [Boston] 1713.

1635   *The Controversie Concerning Liberty of Conscience in Matters of Religion.* London, 1646, 1649. First published in Roger Williams, *The Bloudy Tenent of Persecution.* London, 1644.

1636   *A Letter of Mr. John Cottons . . . to Mr. Williams. . . .* London, 1643.

1636   *The True Constitution Of A particular visible Church, proved by Scripture.* London, 1642. Reprinted as *The Doctrine of the Church, To which is committed the Keyes of the Kingdome of Heaven.* London, 1643, 1644.

1636   *A Sermon . . . Deliver'd at Salem, 1636.* Boston, 1713.

1636   *The New Covenant . . . Being the substance of sundry Sermons.* London, 1654. Reprinted as part of *The Covenant of Grace.* London, 1655. Reedited and published as *A Treatise of the Covenant of Grace.* London, 1659, 1671.

1636   *An Abstract, or the Lawes of New England, as they are now established.* London, 1641, reprinted with Scriptural quotations, as *An Abstract of Laws and Government.* London, 1655.

1637   *A Coppy of A Letter of Mr. Cotton of Boston.* [London] 1641.

1637   *A Discourse about Civil Government in a New Plantation Whose Design is Religion.* Cambridge [Mass.], 1663.

1637   *Sixteene Questions of Serious and Necessary Consequence.* London, 1644. Reprinted as *Severall Questions of Serious and Necessary Consequence.* London, 1647.

1637   *A Conference Mr. John Cotton held at Boston.* London, 1646. Reprinted as *Gospel Conversion.* London, 1646.

1639-   *An Exposition upon The Thirteenth Chapter of the Revelation.*
1640   London, 1655, 1656.

1641   *The Powrring out of the Seven Vials.* London, 1642, 1645.

1641   *The Churches Resurrection.* London, 1642.

1641   *A Brief Exposition With Practical Observations Upon the Whole Book of Canticles. Never before Printed.* London, 1655.

1641   *A Briefe Exposition . . . of Ecclesiates.* London, 1654, 1657; Edinburgh: John Nichol, 1868.

1641   *The Way of the Churches of Christ in New-England.* London, 1645.

1643   *The Keyes Of the Kingdom of Heaven.* London, 1644 (six times); Boston: Tappan and Dennet, 1843.

1643   *The Grounds and Ends of the Baptisme of the Children of the Faithfull.* London, 1647.

1644   *The Covenant of Gods Free Grace.* London, 1645.

1645   *Milk for Babes. Drawn Out of the Breasts of both Testaments.* London, 1646, 1648; Boston, 1656; London, 1668, 1672; Cambridge, Mass., 1691; Boston, 1720, 1747.

1646   *The Bloudy Tenent, Washed and Made White in the Bloud of the Lambe.* London, 1647.

1646   *Singing of Psalmes a Gospel Ordinance.* London, 1647, 1650.
1647   Prefatory Epistle in John Norton, *Responsio ad totam quaestionum syllogen à Guilelmo Apollonio propositam.* London, 1648. Republished in English as *The Answer to the Whole Set of Questions of the Celebrated Mr. William Apollonius.* Cambridge, Mass.: Harvard University Press, 1958.
1647   *The Way of Congregational Churches Cleared.* London, 1648.
1649   *Of the Holinesse of Church Members.* London, 1650.
1651. *A Defence of Mr. John Cotton From the imputation of Selfe Contradiction.* Oxford, 1658.
1651   *Certain Queries Tending to Accommodation and Communion of Presbyterian & Congregational Churches.* London, 1654.
1651   Prefatory Epistle in John Norton, *The Orthodox Evangelist.* London, 1654.

B. *Published Letters*

1626   (Boston, May 31) To James Ussher, Archbishop of Armagh, concerning his treatise on predestination. Published in *The Whole Works of the Most Rev. James Ussher, D.D.,* ed. Charles R. Elrington. Dublin: Hodges, 1864, XV, 330-31.
1632   (October 3) To his wife, Sarah Story Cotton. Published in *Chronicles of the First Planters of the Colony of Massachusetts Bay,* ed. Alexander Young. Boston: C. C. Little & J. Brown, 1846, pp. 432-33.
1633   (May 7) To Dr. John Williams, Bishop of Lincoln, resigning his vicarship in Williams' diocese. Published in *Chronicles,* ed. Young, pp. 434-37.
1634   (Boston, December 3) To a Puritan minister in England, regarding Cotton's reasons for moving to New England. Published in *Chronicles,* ed. Young, pp. 438-44.
1636   "Certain Proposals made by Lord Say, Lord Brooke, and other Persons of quality, as conditions of their removing to New England, with the answers thereto." Published in Thomas Hutchinson, *The History of . . . Massachusetts Bay.* London, 1764, and Hutchinson, *History,* ed. Lawrence S. Mayo. Cambridge, Mass: Harvard University Press, 1936, I, 410-13.
1636   "Copy of a Letter from Mr. Cotton to Lord Say and Seal in the year 1636." Published in Hutchinson, *History,* ed. Mayo, I, 414-17.

Many unpublished letters are in the Prince Collection of the Boston Public Library. Robert Scholz is preparing an edition.

C. *Published Poems.*

before Lines describing an extreme Puritan (a fragment). Quoted
1620 in William Coddington, *A Demonstration of True Love unto the Rulers of the Colony of the Massachusetts.* n.p., 1674, p. 20.

1633 "Another poem . . . upon his removal from Boston to this Wilderness." Published in John Norton, *Abel being Dead yet Speaketh.* London, 1658, pp. 29-30. Omitted from edition of Boston, 1834. More than half is quoted by Larzer Ziff, *The Career of John Cotton.* Princeton: Princeton University Press, 1962, pp. 164-65.

1647 "On my Reverend and dear Brother Mr. Thomas Hooker." Published in Thomas Hooker, *A Survey of the Summe of Church–Discipline.* London, 1648, preface; in Nathaniel Morton, *New Englands Memoriall.* Cambridge, Mass., 1669; New York, 1937; in George Leon Walker, *History of the First Church in Hartford, 1633-1883.* Hartford: Brown and Gross, 1884, p. 428.

1649 "In Saram," "In Rolandum," "In Utrumque." Published in Cotton Mather, *Magnalia Christi Americana.* London, 1702, III, 31; and subsequent editions.

1651 "To my Reverend Brother Mr. Samuel Stone, Teacher of the Church at Hartford." Published in Samuel Stone, *A Congregational Church Is a Catholike Visible Church.* London, 1652, preface; in G. L. Walker, *History,* pp. 443-44.

1652 "A thankful Acknowledgment of God's Providence." Published in Norton, *Abel,* pp. 28-29; quoted complete in Ziff, *Cotton,* p. 255.

SECONDARY SOURCES

A. *About Cotton*

ADAMS, CHARLES F. *Three Episodes of Massachusetts History.* 2 vols. Boston: Houghton, Mifflin, and Company, 1892. Deals with Anne Hutchinson episode. Largely superseded by Battis (below).

BATTIS, EMERY. *Saints and Sectaries: Anne Hutchinson and the Antinomian Controversy in the Massachusetts Bay Colony.* Chapel Hill: University of North Carolina Press, 1962. A fresh and valuable study, with considerable focus on Cotton. Provides information not readily found elsewhere concerning life in Cotton's Boston and the ways of his church.

CALDER, ISABEL M. "The Authorship of *A Discourse About Civil Government,*" *American Historical Review,* XXXVII (1932), 267-69. Rightly identifies Cotton as the author.

—————. "John Cotton and the New Haven Colony," *New England Quarterly*, III (1930), 82-94. Describes Cotton's dealings with Davenport and the use of *An Abstract of Laws* by the New Haven Colony.

—————. "John Cotton's 'Moses His Judicials,'" *Pubs. Col. Soc. Mass.*, XXVIII (1930-33), 86-94. Good study of the background and influence of Cotton's *An Abstract of Laws*.

COME, DONALD R. "John Cotton, Guide of the Chosen People." Unpublished dissertation, Princeton, 1949. Full, sound study of Cotton's life with some attention to his works.

DEXTER, HENRY MARTIN. *The Congregationalism of the Last Three Hundred Years*. New York: Harper and Brothers, 1800. Though largely superseded by Perry Miller's studies, Dexter provides a broad context for Cotton's career.

FORD, WORTHINGTON C. "Cotton's 'Moses his Judicials,'" *Proc. Mass. Hist. Soc.*, 2nd series, XVI (1903), 274-84. Provides a text of Cotton's defense of his *Abstract*.

GORDON, ALEXANDER. "John Cotton," *Dictionary of National Biography*, XXII, 492-95. An excellent study, often overlooked because of its place in a supplement.

HARASZTI, ZOLTAN. *The Enigma of the Bay Psalm Book*. Chicago: University of Chicago Press, 1956. Shows Cotton to be the author of the preface and argues that he prepared the translation of some psalms, including Psalm 23.

HIRSCH, ELIZABETH. "John Cotton and Roger Williams: Their Controversy Concerning Religious Liberty," *Church History*, X (1941), 38-51. Provides a historical perspective on the debate; not entirely favorable to Williams.

HORNBERGER, THEODORE. "Puritanism and Science: The Relationship Revealed in the Writings of John Cotton," *New England Quarterly*, X (1937), 503-15. Shows Cotton's scientific knowledge to be largely medieval.

MATHER, COTTON. *Magnalia Christi Americana*. London, 1702. Contains an important biography of Cotton.

MILLER, PERRY. *Orthodoxy in Massachusetts, 1630-1650*. Cambridge: Harvard University Press, 1933. Brilliant reconstruction of the development of Massachusetts Bay Congregationalism; Cotton's role is properly emphasized.

MORGAN, EDMUND S. "The Case Against Anne Hutchinson," *New England Quarterly*, X (1937), 635-49. Helpful perspective on Cotton's dealings with Anne Hutchinson.

NORTON, JOHN. *Abel being Dead yet Speaketh*. London, 1658. Abstracted in Samuel Clarke. *A Collection of the Lives of Ten*

Eminent Divines. London, 1662. Reprinted as *Memoir of John Cotton*. Ed. Enoch Pond. Boston: Perkins & Marvin, 1834. Valuable early life by Cotton's successor at the Boston church.

PARKES, HENRY BAMFORD. "John Cotton and Roger Williams Debate Toleration, 1644-1652," *New England Quarterly*, IV (1931), 735-56. Identifies Cotton's view as medieval; Williams' as modern.

POOLE, HARRY A. "The Unsettled Mr. Cotton." Unpublished dissertation, University of Illinois, 1956. Stresses the changes of mind which Cotton underwent.

TUTTLE, JULIUS H. "Writings of Rev. John Cotton." *Bibliographical Essays: A Tribute to Wilberforce Eames*. Cambridge, Mass.: Privately printed, 1924. First-rate listing; very helpful and detailed.

WALKER, WILLISTON. *The Creeds and Platforms of Congregationalism*. New York: C. Scribner, 1893. Very helpful on Cotton's Congregational writings and on the preparation of the Cambridge Platform.

————. *Ten New England Leaders*. New York: Silver, Burdett, and Company, 1901. Contains a good brief biographical study.

WELLES, JUDITH B. "John Cotton, 1584-1652, Churchman and Theologian." Unpublished dissertation, Edinburgh, 1948. First-rate study, especially good for the English years.

WHITING, SAMUEL. "Concerning the Life of the Famous Mr. Cotton, Teacher to the Church of Christ at Boston, in New-England." *Chronicles of the First Planters of the Colony of Massachusetts Bay*. Ed. Alexander Young. Boston: C. C. Little and J. Brown, 1846. Original work of great value. Whiting, minister at Lynn, Massachusetts, provided the skeleton of facts which forms the basis for both Norton's and Mather's biographies.

ZIFF, LARZER. *The Career of John Cotton: Puritanism and the American Experience*. Princeton: Princeton University Press, 1962. The authoritative modern study. May be usefully supplemented by the unpublished dissertations listed here.

————. "The Salem Puritans in the 'Free Aire of a New World,'" *Huntington Library Quarterly*, XX (1957), 373-84. Serves as a useful corrective to the overintellectualization of Miller's study of the origins of American Congregationalism.

B. *Background Information*

ANDREWS, CHARLES M. *The Colonial Period of American History*. Vol. I. New Haven: Yale University Press, 1934.

EMERSON, EVERETT H. "Calvin and Covenant Theology," *Church History*, XXV (1956), 136-44.

Selected Bibliography

————. "John Udall and the Puritan Sermon," *Quarterly Journal of Speech*, XLIV (1958), 282-84.

EUSDEN, JOHN D. *Puritans, Lawyers, and Politics*. New Haven: Yale University Press, 1958.

FLETCHER, HARRIS F. *The Intellectual Development of John Milton*. Vol. II. Urbana: University of Illinois Press, 1961.

GEORGE, CHARLES H. and KATHERINE. *The Protestant Mind of the English Reformation*. Princeton: Princeton University Press, 1961.

HALLER, WILLIAM. *Liberty and Reformation in the Puritan Revolution*. New York: Columbia University Press, 1955.

————. *The Rise of Puritanism*. New York: Columbia University Press, 1938.

HEPPE, HEINRICH. *Reformed Dogmatics*. Trans. G. T. Thomson. London: Allen & Unwin, 1950.

LEVY, BABETTE MAY. *Preaching in the First Half-Century of New England History*. Hartford: The American Society of Church History, 1945.

MILLER, PERRY. "The Marrow of Puritan Divinity," *Pubs. Col. Soc. Mass.*, XXXII (1938), 247-300; reprinted in *Errand into the Wilderness*. Cambridge, Mass.: Harvard University Press, 1956.

————. *The New England Mind: The Seventeenth Century*. Cambridge, Mass.: Harvard University Press, 1954.

————. *The New England Mind: From Colony to Province*. Cambridge, Mass.: Harvard University Press, 1953.

————. *Roger Williams: His Contribution to the American Tradition*. New York: Atheneum Publishers, 1962.

————, and THOMAS H. JOHNSON, eds. *The Puritans*. New York: American Book Company, 1938.

MORGAN, EDMUND S. *The Puritan Dilemma: The Story of John Winthrop*. Boston: Little, Brown, 1958.

————. *The Puritan Family*. Boston: The Trustees of the Public Library, 1944.

MURDOCK, KENNETH. *Literature & Theology in Colonial New England*. New York: Harper and Row, 1963.

PAUCK, WILHELM. *The Heritage of the Reformation*. Glencoe, Illinois: Free Press, 1950.

PORTER, H. C. *Reformation and Reaction in Tudor Cambridge*. Cambridge, Eng.: Cambridge University Press, 1958.

RITSCHL, OTTO. *Dogmengeschichte des Protestantismus*. Vol. III. Göttingen: Vandenhoeck & Ruprecht, 1926.

SASEK, LAWRENCE. *The Literary Temper of the English Puritans*. Baton Rouge: Louisiana State University Press, 1961.

STEARNS, RAYMOND P. *The Strenuous Puritan: Hugh Peter, 1598-1660*. Urbana: University of Illinois Press, 1954.

TRINTERUD, LEONARD J. "The Origins of Puritanism," *Church History*, XX (1951), 37-57.

WEBER, MAX. *The Protestant Ethic and the Spirit of Capitalism.* Trans. Talcott Parsons. London: G. Allen & Unwin, 1930.

WINSLOW, OLA E. *Master Roger Williams.* New York: The Macmillan Company, 1957.

WINTHROP, JOHN. *Journal.* Ed. James K. Hosmer. 2 vols. New York: C. Scribner's Sons, 1908.

Index

Index